CREATING YOUR FIRST SALES TEAM

A Guide for Entrepreneurs, Start-Ups, Small Businesses and Professionals Seeking More Clients and Customers

by Gini Graham Scott, Ph.D.

CREATING YOUR FIRST SALES TEAM

Copyright © 2017 by Gini Graham Scott

TABLE OF CONTENTS

INTRODUCTION

I wrote this book after creating, coordinating, and motivating a small sales team to represent me at the American Film Market or AFM for short. For me it was a new experience, after writing 150 books and working mainly on my own, though I have had some part-time students, moms, and even a few professionals seeking spare income to assist with database, editorial, and assorted administrative tasks. But never a sales team. Before then, I got leads from assorted business and professional organizations I belong to, such as several local Chambers of Commerce, business referral groups, and writers associations.

The, I decided I needed a team of sales reps to represent me by contacting exhibitors and attendees at the biggest trade show for the film industry -- the American Film Market. Though I have gone to some of these big trade events before and learned how to be successful at cold calling and making elevator pitches, this year, I didn't want to go for many reasons. Among other things, it would mean spending a day going to and returning from L.A., setting up meetings in advance, and giving up a week of paid work writing for clients.

So the more I thought about going there, I realized I could be much more effective if I could put together a small team of people to represent me at the show. Then, I could coordinate things from my house via email and phone by providing the reps with guidance on who to see, what to say, and what information to get, so I could follow up later with those possibly interested in distributing my film projects or producing or co-producing my scripts.

The result was I recruited a team of three people, and I had to develop all kinds of materials for them, so they would know how to make an initial contact and what they would receive after I did the necessary follow-up to close the sale. These materials included agreements, an outline of commissions, guidelines on who to contact, and what to say and do. Plus I had to make initial contacts by email with prospects and make referrals to the rep who would be at the show that day. Additionally, I had to provide them with forms to keep track of who they contacted from my referrals, as well as from the leads they developed at the show.

The outcome was very successful, resulting in some strong potential film sales and big commissions to the reps who made those contacts. This outcome led me to think that I could share what I learned about creating one's first sales team with others, since I found no book on the subject from a search of sales teams and sales management books on Amazon. The books on the subject were all directed towards the sales manager or company owner who is coordinating a large sales team. But there was nothing for the entrepreneur, start-up, small business, or professional seeking the first or two, three, or four reps.

Thus, I have written this book for them, based on my experience and that of several business owners and professionals who have gotten a few reps to help them grow their business. I have included examples of the materials I developed to sign-up, coordinate, and motivate my team, which you can use as a guide or feel free to adapt for your own purposes.

The topics covered include the following:
- Determining when you need a sales rep to represent you
- Finding prospective sales reps
- Recruiting sales reps on different platforms
- Explaining the requirements and interview prospective reps
- Assessing skills and getting references
- Developing guidelines for what sales reps should say and do
- Creating commission arrangements and contracts
- Hiring reps as independent contractors and avoiding employment law
    issues
- Creating reporting documents to know what reps have done to follow up
- Coordinating reps in the field by email and phone
- Assigning responsibilities to sales team members
- Dealing with reps who don't perform and reassigning duties to other reps
- Having a debriefing with reps
- Organizing the information from your reps for follow up
- Figuring out commissions and making payments

So now, good luck, and may you have success in bringing aboard your first sales reps or small team to represent you.

PART I: FINDING AND HIRING YOUR REPS

CHAPTER 1: DECIDING WHEN YOU NEED A SALES REP OR TEAM TO REPRESENT YOU

Deciding to hire your first sales rep or a small team of reps is a critical decision, because it can change the nature of your business or businesses.

The usual reason for bringing in a sales rep or reps is you want more work or don't like the marketing and sales process, so you hope to delegate this task to someone else. In either case, you are launching a new type of business. You are not only potentially bringing in more work or using an intermediary to deal with your clients or customers, but now you have to develop guidelines and procedures for working with your rep or reps. So you have to find time to create these materials and deal with your reps, in addition to the work you regularly do.

On the other hand, if you want to expand and perhaps move into managing the work with additional employees, starting out with a few sales reps is a good way to build your business.

The Difference between Sales Reps and Using a Service for Getting Clients or Referrals and Leads through Networking

In many industries, there are services you can sign up with to get leads. Then, you deal directly with the leads and compensate the service through a monthly or yearly membership fee, or you pay a pitch fee for each pitch you make. For example, as a writer, I belong to many groups that provide leads in that industry, such as the Association of Ghostwriters, American Society of Journalists and Authors, and Writers and Editors Network, which provide listings of new projects where clients are seeking writers. Plus there are some book packaging companies that are looking for writers for their clients' projects.

If I see a posting that looks interesting, I will respond, and there may be a fee for making the pitch or a commission for a lead that turns into a client. In other cases, members can access a jobs forum for information on new writing projects, and a member can freely contact the person offering the work at no charge. But this process is more akin to responding to newspaper and online ads for work; you don't have anyone making the connections for you. Rather, you are getting leads from third parties, but you aren't hiring anyone to get these leads for you.

Hiring a rep or small sales team is also different from expanding your business through business referral, networking, or partners groups. Sometimes at these meetings, the organizers describe the other group members as akin to having a sales force out there representing you. The groups also provide a forum for informing others about what you do, so they can bring you referrals and leads. The referrals are more like personal introductions, where the group member is proactive in connecting you and the person referred to you, such as by sending out an introduction email or by asking you to report back on the results of your following up with that referral. By contrast, a lead is more like giving you a suggested contact who might be interested in your products or services. But in either case, the person is voluntarily giving you a referral or lead. There is no arrangement between you and the person giving you the lead, even if you offer a small commission -- say 10% -- to anyone giving you the name of someone to contact, which I occasionally offer. However, any such referrals or leads are sporadic, and you have no formal agreement.

Thus, even if you provide others in the group with your sales literature or do a short presentation about what you do and the kinds of clients or customers you want, any referrals or leads are hit or miss. Some group members may know possible customers or clients for you, or maybe not. Likewise, if you go to afterhours mixers, business support groups, or mastermind meetings, you may find prospective customers or clients or referrals to other prospects, but this isn't the same as creating a sales team.

Certainly, getting referrals or leads in these ways is a good idea, and you may find these organizations and groups a very effective means of getting more customers and clients, building your business, and increasing your income. In fact, if your business is growing enough in this way, you may not need to hire a sales rep or sales team, unless you want to grow even more. Or you might want to bring in a rep or a team to help with part of your business or by attending a particular event for you, as I have done.

In short, bringing in a sales rep or reps to build your business or represent you at an event is different from using a third party or participating at a business meeting or event to provide you with leads. These can all be great ways of building your business. But a sales rep or team can help by directly providing outreach for you on a project, event, or ongoing basis.

Deciding to Hire a Sales Rep or Create a Small Sales Team

Following are some considerations about whether to hire a sales rep or team and for what purpose.

- Do you want to truly expand to another level, which means that you will be become a sales manager or will you need someone to manage your sales team? Or do you want to bring in a sales rep or team to represent you on an occasional basis for a special event or events?

- Do you want a rep or team to be familiar with your field or industry? Or is having prior knowledge less necessary, since you can handle the needed training?

- Is it okay for a rep or team to represent other products or services in your field, so they can offer your product or service, too, such as when an insurance agent represents a number of companies with different services and plans? Or do you want a rep or team to only represent your product or service when they contact prospects?

- Can you provide sales reps with the necessary knowledge and literature to give out to present your product or service to others? Are you interested in providing the training personally or through a training manual, video, emails, or other materials?

- Will you follow up on sales leads to close the deal, or do you expect your sales reps to take the orders and close the deals themselves?

- Can you a put together the necessary contracts or agreements to spell out what the rep will do and what compensation -- commonly a commission or draw and commissions - the rep will receive for closing a deal or bringing you a contact that leads to closed business?

- Do you have a product or service that provides a sufficient commission or royalty to appeal to a sales rep? Or does representing you open doors to an industry the rep wants to learn about and enter?

- Do you have the time and interest to expand your business in this way?

In short, ask yourself a series of questions to clarify what you want the sales rep or team to do and determine if you have an attractive enough offer for someone to be interested in representing your product or service. Also, decide if you really want to invest the time and effort to create, recruit, and support a sales rep or reps. You are not just hiring someone to bring you new clients or customers. But you are taking your business in a whole new direction.

Finally, when you bring in a sales rep, you have to understand the employment laws so you know the difference between hiring the reps as independent contractors and employees. You want to start by bringing in reps as independent contractors working for you on an occasional and part-time basis where they are working independently. Otherwise, you will open yourself to a whole series of requirements, including paying fees for workers comp, insurance, and taxes. Of course, as your business grows, hiring employees is something to consider, when you have a larger sales team and you have more control and supervision over what the reps do on a part-time or fulltime basis. But I don't recommend this when you are starting out with your first sales rep or reps.

So I recommend starting off by hiring independent contractors and following the guidelines, so they are clearly and legally working for you in this capacity. You can also decide whether to hire sales reps on a commission only or draw against commission basis, as will be discussed.

Now if you are still determined to hire your first sales reps, read on about how to recruit them and then train and guide them, so they know what to do.

CHAPTER 2: FINDING PROSPECTIVE SALES REPS

Once you decide to create a sales team, the next step is finding prospective reps. As part of this process, you need to provide them with materials to explain what you are selling, as well as show them what they will present to prospects in order to sell your products or services. You also need to have contracts or agreement forms to indicate more formally what you expect of them and what they will be getting in return.

But before you get into all that, you can start with some initial prospecting to determine if working for you appeals to any prospective reps who are interested in learning more. I'll cover what you need to show prospective reps in the following chapters. Here I'll focus on where to find such reps and what to tell them to gain their interest and decide if they seem to be likely candidates for representing you.

Where to Find Reps

You can find reps in numerous places. A good place to start before placing ads for jobs is where you already have personal connections, such as through business networking and referral groups, through Meetup groups, where you are a member or organizer, or through a local online forum, such as a Next Door neighborhood group. Place an announcement, then follow up with more details to those who are interested. This is how I found reps to work with on two different projects. Here are more details on using these different approaches.

Family Members, Relatives and Friends

Depending on the interest of family members, relatives, and friends, this could be a good starting point. They may not be interested themselves -- and often that's a good thing, so you don't mix the personal with business, but they may know people who might be interested in being a rep for you. For example, they might know professionals or college students looking for part-time work and refer you to them or tell them to contact you.

Business Networking and Referral Groups

Business and networking groups take numerous forms, and if you already belong to one or more groups, great. Otherwise, consider joining groups in your area for the business community as a whole or for individuals in your profession, trade, or industry. Some of these groups might include:

- <u>Chambers of Commerce</u> in your community and surrounding areas. Some of these have business partner groups for making referrals to each other, regular afterhours mixers, and workshops and seminars on business marketing. Commonly, these business partner groups meet once a month or every two weeks.

- <u>Business Networking International (BNI) chapters</u>. Usually you can go as a visitor or guest to any local chapter, if you are not already a member. As part of the meeting, members, and sometimes guests and visitors in non-competing professions, get to give a 30-second announcement about what they do and what kinds of referrals they are looking for. A part of the meeting is also devoted to one or two 7 to 10 minute presentations by members about their business, power partners, and types of referrals they are seeking. Plus members are encouraged to set up one-on-one meetings. The groups are limited to one person per profession.

- <u>Business to Business Referral Groups</u>. These groups typically meet once a month and follow a similar format of short pitches of about 30-60 seconds by members, 7-10 minute presentations by one to three members, and a time for special announcements. Commonly, the group is limited to one person per profession, and members are encouraged to set up small meetings outside the regular meeting, sometimes by counting off by numbers to end up with groups of 3, and sometimes 2 or 4 people.

- <u>Business Networking Groups</u>. These groups are open to any businesses; they are not limited by the one person per profession rule. In some groups, the meeting starts with sharing business cards and 30-60 second introductions, and then everyone breaks up into pairs or small groups for networking for about 30-40 minutes. Sometimes there will be a time for announcements or participants can include this with their announcement. And some groups may combine introductions with one or two presentations by speakers on ways to be successful in one's business. The formats vary, but a key component is networking and making connections to get more business.

- <u>Professional, Trade, and Interest Groups</u>. Whatever your profession, trade, or interest, you will find groups to match. Sometimes these groups have workshops and seminars on how to improve your business, as well as regular or occasional networking events.

Such groups can provide an ideal source of prospective reps for certain industries. You have to fit the type of rep you are looking for to the businesses and interests of people in the group.

For example, after I created a series of books on personality typing by dividing people into four main personality types based on four popular dogs in a Dog Type system, rather than letters, terms, and colors as in other popular systems, I found a relationships coach who wanted to lead my program. He was already the group leader, and to gain his interest, I showed off the books I had written and described how I planned to create a workshop program and was looking for workshop leaders. The coach was interested, and after we met, I created some additional materials for conducting the program. I started by creating some handouts from charts in the book, and eventually I developed some questionnaires, evaluation forms, guidelines for what to say, suggested exercises, and more. In addition, the coach developed an outline for his presentation and posters of the four dogs, so participants could get into groups based on their personality type . Eventually, all of these materials became part of a workbook on conducting a workshop; and later, I recorded the first three workshop and turned the transcripts into a guidebook for conducting a workshop. Later, another coach in St. Louis who liked the program was able to use these materials to conduct workshops there. So now the basic materials are in place for reaching out to other prospective trainers for the program.

Here's an example of what you might say in a 30 second announcement, since these groups have guidelines in what to say, followed by a sample announcement by me to get a rep.   If you only get 15 seconds as a guest or visitor, shorten your pitch to the bare essentials. You can use the following template as a guide:

Hi…
I'm NAME from YOUR COMPANY NAME. We WHAT YOU DO OR SPECIALIZE IN TO HELP OTHERS GAIN WHAT BENEFIT. Today, I'm looking for/Who do you know NOW EXPLAIN WHAT KIND OF REP YOU ARE LOOKING FOR TO DO WHAT WHEN -- AND BY WHEN DO YOU NEED THE PROSPECT TO CONTACT YOU. You can learn more about my company YOUR COMPANY NAME at YOUR WEBSITE, EMAIL, AND/OR PHONE NUMBER). And my PowerPartners are (LIST 3 OR 4 TYPES OF COMPANIES THAT MIGHT BE LIKELY TO GIVE YOU REFERRALS OR WORK WITH YOU)

Here's how I created a pitch based on the template:

Hi…

I'm Gini Graham Scott of Changemakers Publishing and Writing. We specialize in writing books, articles, blogs, and other materials to help clients gain more visibility, credibility, and authority to get more customers, clients and sales. Today, I'm looking for 2-3 reps for a big film trade show, the American Film Market on November 1 to 8 in Santa Monica. The reps will meet with potential distributors, sales agents, producers, and others who might be interested in distributing our completed film or co-producing our future films. They'll get a commission on sales, and I'll provide full guidelines and sales materials, and follow-up on any leads.

If you go to networking events, you can use a similar pitch when you meet people. Just make it sound more conversational, and adapt the length of what you say to the situation. Keep it short and compact, and if the person you are talking to seems interested, you can expand on your opening pitch. Also, show interest in whatever the other person is doing, and if possible, let the other person speak first, so you know what he or she does and is interested in. This way, you can adapt your pitch to the other person's interests.

Meetup and Interest Groups

Meetup groups focused around a particular industry or interest related to your business can be another source for finding reps. So can interest groups whether local or online, especially if you are the organizer or leader of the group, since that gives you more credibility and authority than if you are just a member. Also, as a leader or organizer, you can email everyone in the group to announce what you are looking for, whereas if just a member, you may not be able to email everyone and can only post to a discussion group if there is one.

That's how I found three team members to go to the American Film Market (AFM) in Santa Monica from November 1 to 8. I decided I didn't want to go myself for various reasons, as previously noted in the introduction. Yet I wanted to have a presence there in order to pitch completed films to distributor and scripts and documentaries to producers and co-producers.

After deciding I wanted some sales reps at the event, I invited members of four groups where I am an organizer -- two based in L.A. that I took over when I lived there for two years (the Film and TV Connection and the Hollywood Film Industry), and the others based in the Bay Area, modeled after the L.A. groups (the Bay Area Film and TV Connection and the San Francisco Film Industry).

Combined, they have about10,000 members, and I thought they were an ideal target group for my ads for a rep at a film industry show in L.A.

Though I hadn't set up a meeting or sent out an announcement to these groups for several months, I sent out a series of email pitches to the groups, indicating that I was looking for individuals to go to the AFM. I explained that I needed someone who would be getting a pass to the show for at least one day, since they would be meeting with exhibitors in hotel rooms and by a pool that was restricted to attendees with a badge for that day or for the show. I also explained what they would be doing, and I asked those interested to email me for further information, whereupon I sent them some introductory material and later sent other supporting material over the next few weeks. I was most interested in talking to individuals who already wanted to go to the show to pitch their own material or wanted to learn how to prepare to attend the AFM in the future. I'll discuss the materials I provided in a subsequent chapter.

Following are the series of announcements I sent. I got a few interested contacts after each mailing, and eventually I spoke to about a dozen potential candidates. I winnowed the respondents down to eliminate those who weren't interested or who had limited experience presenting anything to anyone. I was most interested in meeting individuals who had experience in sales. While some individuals realized that they didn't have the time, interest, or ability to do this, finally the process yielded three interested individuals, although one of them later flamed out at the show, as I'll describe in a future chapter.

Here are the emails I sent over several weeks to find these reps:

September 28, 2017
Subject Line: Earn Money at the AFM, 1 or 2 More Opportunities to Be Part of Psychological Thriller with Name Actors
Hi All…
Earn Money at the AFM in November
Are you going to the AFM (American Film Market) in Santa Monica Nov. 1-8? We are looking for one or two people who might like to join with us in presenting our slate of 4 film projects to distributors and 4 additional scripts for co-production or production deals. You will receive a finders/referral fee, as well as Associate, Co-Producer, or Executive Producer credits depending on how much you raise… Let me know by email if you are interested, and I can send you more information on our slate of films and scripts. When you write, tell me a little about yourself, your past experience with sales, promotion, making presentations, or pitching film projects. If you have a link to a website, please include that, along with a phone number and the best times to call. You can email me at giniscott@sbcglobal.net.

October 14, 2017

Subject Line: Final Notice: Earn Money at the AFM, 1 or 2 More Opportunities to Be Part of a Psychological Thriller with Name Actors Since Filming Postponed Due to Las Vegas Shooting

Hi All…

Earn Money at the AFM in November

Are you going to the AFM (American Film Market) in Santa Monica Nov. 1-8? We are looking for one more person to join us in presenting our slate of 4 film projects to distributors and 4 additional scripts and 2 documentaries for co-production or production deals. You need to have or get a ticket to the AFM for at least 1 day. You will receive a finders/referral fee, as well as Associate, Co-Producer, or Executive Producer credits depending on how much you raise. You will join a team of 2 other reps at the AFM, and I will send you guidelines on what to do. I will be dividing up the exhibitors/distributors/sales agents to contact alphabetically or by floor, and then I will follow-up to close the deals. Let me know by email if you are interested, and be sure to include your phone number. I can send you more information on our slate of films and scripts. When you write, tell me a little about yourself, your past experience with sales, promotion, making presentations, or pitching film projects. If you have a link to a website, include that. You can rep these projects along with anything else you are doing at the AFM. You can email me at giniscott@sbcglobal.net.

October 26, 1017

Subject Line: Team at the AFM, 1 or 2 More Opportunities to Be Part of a Psychological Thriller with Name Actors

Hi All…

Team at the AFM in November

We are delighted to announce we will have 3 team members at the AFM presenting our slate of films to distributors and sales agents and our scripts and documentary proposals to producers and production companies. Many thanks to this group for responding to my announcement about being part of this team a few weeks ago. More news after the show, along with the next films we will be producing.

November 3, 2017
Subject Line: Update on AFM Meetings, Last Opportunity to Be Part of a Psychological Thriller with Name Actors
Hi All…
Update at the AFM in November
This has been a fantastic year at the AFM, which started 3 days ago. The directors/producers of our *Infidelity* film and five others together have had about 20 meetings to set up distribution for *Infidelity* and three other current projects. Meanwhile, our reps will be going to about 25 meetings we already scheduled with distributors, sales agents, producers, and other film industry professionals. Then, we'll be following up along with the directors/producers.

Again, thanks to the members of our various meet up groups for responding about being part of this team. More details on our next slate of films -- two sci-fi films and an action thriller -- and how you can participate in a couple of weeks.

Advertising and Announcements for a Rep

Another way to find a rep is to advertise or announce this locally. There are three ways to do this: through a local community forum like Next Door, an advertising vehicle such as Craigslist, or a neighborhood bulletin board.

Ideally, find someone in your area who you can meet with personally, although given the power of the Internet and social media, you can hire someone in another area, especially if your target market includes that area or if an event, such as a trade show, will be in that location. Another source for reps might be the business management or marketing department or the placement office at a local college or university.

Here are some suggestions on where to advertise or post an announcement for a rep.

Posting on Next Door

Next Door is a great resource, since it is an online forum for neighborhoods, and you can probably find one for your community, since there are 158,000 neighborhoods around the U.S.
You just need to sign-up to be connected to others within a certain radius of your location. Their website is https://nextdoor.com/find-neighborhood. For example, I'm in the Trails Area in Lafayette, which includes about 1200 local neighbors and about 14,000 residents in 47 nearby neighborhoods. People can post all sorts of things, from lost dogs and cats to information on Internet outages;

recommendations of local business; requests for doctors, dentists, and other professionals; and reports of recent property thefts and accidents. Plus if you are looking for help in a particular area, such as a sales rep, this is a great way to connect with your neighbors at no charge, and you may find just the right person in your own neighborhood.

For example, I have repeatedly used Next Door to find independent contractors to work on various projects. For the past three years, I used it to find local students, moms, and a radio journalist to assist with different work tasks. I also posted an announcement for illustrators for a kids' book and got a dozen responses, resulting in my signing up three illustrators to illustrate three kids' books I wrote. I've seen many other people post offers for part-time employees. So it works.

Placing an Ad or Announcement on Craigslist

Craigslist (www.craigslist.org) is another place to find sales reps. You can post the work as a gig for a short-term or part-time opportunity or a job if you expect this to be a longer term arrangement. Normally, you use Craigslist to post in and around your own city, although I know some people who used it for long-distance recruitment, such as some filmmakers in one city looking for talent and crew to film in another part of the country.

If you have a paid job or gig, you can post in different categories, though each category has a posting fee, which ranges from $7 to $75, depending on where you ae posting the ad. Generally, if you are posting in a metropolitan area like San Francisco, figure on $75 per category. For a sales rep position, you might post this in the business/management or customer service jobs category. Or if this is a gig, the most relevant category might be "event."

You can also post on Craigslist for free in the community category under gigs, and limit the job to a particular category or to all, which might be a good idea, since this job could appeal to people from all types of backgrounds who are looking for short-term or part-time work. Commonly, your post will stay up for 30 days if it's a job, or 30-45 days if it's a gig, depending on the city.

I know many people who successfully used Craigslist to get actors and crew members for film projects; other people got tenants for their homes or apartments. However, you have to be careful in screening respondents, since sometimes you can set up appointments and people don't show up, as I found when I lived in San Francisco for two years and advertised for actors for a short volunteer film project. Then, too, Craigslist is sometimes used for scams, where people go to meet respondents to their ad and get robbed.

Thus, if you use Craigslist, take some time to talk to whoever expresses interest and check out any references, along with their website or Facebook page.

Spend a little extra time with a referral through Craigslist to make sure they are responsible, reliable, and legit, and take time to talk to them on the phone to explain what you expect them and what experience they have had in doing similar work in the past to qualify them -- a topic discussed further on interviewing prospective reps.

Posting on Neighborhood Bulletin Boards or Display Tables

Local bulletin boards or display tables can be another source of finding reps. Choose a few places with bulletin boards or display tables where people are actively posting notices and checking current postings. Some likely places include your local supermarket, library, or community center. Commonly, you can post a flyer or put it on the display table along with other postings or display materials. But sometimes you need to get an approval from whoever is in charge of these bulletin boards and tables. If so, you'll usually see a check mark and initials on the material posted or displayed. If any permission is required or you aren't sure, check with the person in charge about what you want to promote for their approval. Otherwise, you are likely to find your material removed and you may not be able to post or display in the future.

Contacting Your Local Colleges and Universities

Sometimes college or university students may be a good fit with your prospective sales team, especially those majoring in business and interested in marketing and sales. To appeal to such students, contact the Department of Business Administration. Or if you are recruiting sales reps for a particular type of event, students in a related department might be interested. For instance, if you are looking for sales reps to pitch a health product or service, try contacting the Health Sciences or Nursing Department. If you are representing a travel program, contact the Department of Recreation and Tourism. Additionally, you can list your sales opportunity with the college placement department. To find out who to contact, call the central number for the campuses near you and ask to contact particular departments and the placement office.

Creating a Recruitment Plan

Obviously, you won't have the time or ability to use all of these avenues to find reps. So work out a plan for what types of connections you want to make. Then, list the different approaches you might consider using and prioritize them, so you can use your highest priority recruitment approaches first.

You can use the chart on the following page to rank the approaches described in this chapter and add others that appeal to you. Also, prepare the materials you need to promote your sales opportunity and present them to those who respond to your ad or announcement.

RECRUITMENT PLAN		
Recruitment Approach	**Rating (from 1-10)**	**Ranking/Priority (from 1-5)**
Family Members and Relatives		
Friends		
Business Networking and Referral Groups (Chambers of Commerce, BNI, B2B, BNF, and other groups)		
Trade and Professional Groups		
Meetup Groups		
Interest Groups		
Advertising and Announcements (Next Door, Craigslist)		
Posting on Neighborhood Bulletin Boards and Display Tables		
Other		

As you get responses, keep track of where they come from, so as needed you can continue using that approach, such as by putting up another post on Next Door or putting out more flyers at another event. If you still need more leads, try your next highest ranked approach.

Once you start to get responses from likely candidates, you can decide on the best ones to join your reps.

What if you aren't getting responses? Or what if the responses are from individuals who don't have the necessary sales skills? In either case, reconsider both your offering for a rep and your approach to advertising your offer. Maybe you aren't clear in what you are offering. Maybe you are not providing a large enough incentive for representing you. Maybe you are posting your information about the project in the wrong forums. Or maybe your offering isn't getting out to your audience.

There could be any number of possible problems, and it can be hard to determine exactly what the problem is. But consider different possibilities, and change your approach to get a rep accordingly.

In the worst case scenario where you can't find a rep, continue to work as your own sales rep. This way you build up a track record of getting sales and have a better understanding of what might appeal to prospective reps. And perhaps after some time, you will have more to sell and your products and services will have an increased appeal to potential reps. Then, with this new knowledge and experience you have gained, try building your team again, and this time, you are more likely to be successful, since you now know so much more.

CHAPTER 3: ORGANZING YOUR SALES MATERIALS

To help you recruit, guide, and motivate your team, you need to create a variety of sales materials. You need three types of materials:

- Announcements, ads, flyers, and other materials to recruit sales reps,
- Flyers, promotional information, and other materials to help your sales reps pitch your program and make sales,
- Background information on you and your company to show your authority and credibility.

While the materials to recruit your sales reps is only for this purpose, the sales and promotional material will help prospective sales reps decide to rep you, based on seeing how you are supporting them with your sales literature. Then, if they rep you, they can use that material to show to prospective clients. At the same time, you have to give reps information about your past track record, so they feel you are a solid businessperson and you will honor your agreements to pay them the commissions that are due.

Creating Materials to Recruit Your Sales Reps

Announcements

Just as I used announcements to my film Meetup groups to recruit sales reps for the AFM conference, you can create your own announcements to find reps. In these announcements, briefly describe what kind of reps you are seeking, what they will be doing, and what they will receive in return. Such announcements can go to a group you are running or can post these announcements, or you can put them in a newsletter to send to your email list. Ideally, you already have such a list. If not, there are many courses, books, and articles on how to create such a list.

Adapt the announcement to appeal to your audience. You can use examples of previous announcements sent to group members as a guide in deciding what to say and the usual length of these announcements. Based on my experience in getting reps, these are the key subjects to cover:

- <u>a strong direct headline indicating what you are looking for and when</u>
  (ie: Earn Money at the AFM in November)

- <u>a direct appeal to your target prospects</u>, and perhaps include any qualifying characteristics of the rep you are seeking to exclude those who don't meet this criteria

(ie: Are you going to the AFM (American Film Market Nov. 1-8)

- <u>a description of what you are looking for</u>, including what you expect the person to do.

(ie: We are looking for one or two people who might like to join us in presenting our slate of 4 film projects to distributors and 4 additional scripts for co-production or production deals)

- <u>a brief description of what the rep will get in return for repping you</u>

(ie: You will receive a finders/referral fee, as well as Associate, Co-Producer, or Executive Producer credits, depending on what you do)

- <u>an indication of the likely success of their efforts</u>

(ie: We have already found a distributor for our first film and have several distributors who have already expressed interest in our new films, so you are likely to find a receptive audience…or….We have already created 6 films , so we already have a track record of success you can build on)

- <u>an explanation about how prospects can get more information about what they will be doing and the sales opportunity</u>

(ie: Let me know by email if you are interested, and I can send you more information on our slate of films and scripts.)

- <u>a description of how they should respond and what information they should provide to show their level of interest, past experience, and how you can contact them</u>

(ie: When you write, tell me a little about yourself, your past experience with sales, promotion, making presentations, or pitching film projects. If you have a link to a website, include that. Please include a phone number, too, and the best times to call. You can email me at …)

Those are the basic elements. Adapt what you say to prospective reps, so you emphasize what would appeal to them about the opportunity and how they will find success in representing you, not only for this project but in other ways of working for you.

Ads

These are short little blurbs to let people know you are looking for reps to represent you, and they include a link for more information. If you have a relevant photo to include, do so, because research shows that readers are more likely to read ads with images.

You don't need to pay for these ads. Instead, post them in your social media accounts, such as on Twitter, Facebook, and LinkedIn, and in any online groups you belong to where participants might be interested in being a rep. For

Twitter, figure on ads being 140 characters (or possibly 280 characters), and now photos can be included without being deducted from your character count. For Facebook and LinkedIn, your ad can be a little longer - say up to 400 characters.

As an example, an ad might read something like this, with a link to learn more:

140 characters: "Earn money at AFM as our sales rep for films. Meet distributors, agents, producers. Details: www.newfilms.com or salesrep@newfilms.com,"

300 characters: "Are you going to the AFM? Want to earn money and meet distributors, sales agents, and producers? We're looking for 2 or 3 sales reps to represent us for our completed films and future projects. For more information, visit our website at www.newfilms.com and email us at salesrep@newfilms.com. "

Flyers

These are one-page pitches to get prospective sales reps to contact you. These are different from any flyers you may give your reps to use when they contact prospective customers or clients. Essentially, these flyers include the same information as an announcement, except you add the element of design to make your pitch for sales reps more visually appealing. You can use these flyers for posters and displays at events, or you can send them as PDFs for initial inquiries, such as when someone contacts you after seeing one of your very short ads.

The following is an example of a flyer that we used for recruiting a sales rep:

WE'RE LOOKING FOR 2-3 SALES REPS

SET UP TALKS AND WORKSHOPS ON OUR UNIQUE PERSONALITY PROFILING SYSTEM

USING THE DOG TYPE PERSONALITY SYSTEM FOR SUCCESS IN YOUR LIFE AND WORK

Meet Our Trainers and Experience an Introductory Workshop

Contact us to attend the next workshop in your area or see a workshop video if out of the area.

The workshop features these topics:
 - Discover your dog type and that of others
 - Better communicate with others
 - Get more customers or clients
- Improve teamwork in your organization
- Get to know others better and have more fun!
The program features a variety of techniques and exercises, and a presentation. 7-7:15 – Networking; 7:30-8:45 - Program; 8:45-9 – More Networking

The Dog Type system builds on other personality profiling methods, like Myers-Briggs, DISC, and red-yellow-blue-green color profiling. But it uniquely uses dogs, where the German Shepherd is the strong leader; the Pomeranian, the high-energy party animal; the Golden Retriever, the calm, steady supporter and helper; and the Border Collie, the serious detail-oriented type concerned with facts and accuracy.

Call 925-385-0608 if interested. To RSVP: Email changemakerspub@att.net or sign up on Meetup at www.meetup.com/whats-your-dog-type.

You can keep these flyers relatively simple, when you are just getting started and are looking for part-time reps interested in a short-term project for some spare income. Later, you can create more professionally designed flyers. For simple flyers, you can readily create them in a Word document with a few different sizes of fonts and some stock images. Or use a template for creating such flyers when you just insert your copy and images, or use a template for creating such flyers, where you insert your copy and images. You can find sources for templates online if you go to "word templates," and Microsoft has free templates if you go to https://templates.office.com/en-us/flyers. With these templates, you can readily make changes, such as for different dates for workshops.

Other Recruitment Materials about Your Program

Besides the announcements, ads, and flyers to get prospective sales reps to call you, you need additional material to show reps what they will be selling. They can also show some of these materials to potential customers and clients. Depending on what they are pitching, they need the following:

- For a product, they need to see the product catalog and one-sheets or a link to a website where these products are for sale.
- For a professional service, they need to see a description of the services offered and the background and expertise of the person providing that service.
- For a program, they need information on what the program provides. If you have a 2-3 minute video featuring highlights of the program, such as someone providing a service or a workshop leader putting on a program, that's ideal. Possibly you can prospective reps to a program if they are in the area.

There are several ways to create a video.

- You can hire a videographer to film the program and edit it to feature the highlights. You might insert some interviews with you and workshop participants, or record a voice-over to explain what's going on. The videographer can edit this together. Figure on about $500-2000 to create such a video.

- Alternatively, create a simple video using photos from the program along with text explaining what is happening. You can use a video creation platform where you insert the slides and text. Some of these platforms are available from Animoto (www.animoto.com) and Video Builder (http://www.videobuilder.io).

- Another way to create a video is to start with a PowerPoint presentation and turn that into a video with PowerPoint10 and above. To do so, go to Add Ons, set up Camtasia, and produce a voice over as you go from slide to slide. At the end, render your completed PowerPoint and voice-over as a video.

Sales Materials Which Sales Reps Will Use to Pitch Your Program

Still another way to help reps understand your products, services, or programs is to provide them with the sales materials they will be using to pitch the program. If you already have the material prepared, that's great. But you can also work on creating these materials while you are in the process of initially contacting prospective sales reps and having initial meetings with them. That's what I did in recruiting three people to represent me at the AFM and in developing an outreach program to bring in sales reps to promote the Dog Type personality program. I also used this recruitment period as a time to find out what sales reps would need to pitch our films at the AFM and to pitch the Dog Type program to prospects in different types of companies and organizations.

Depending on what you are promoting, the kinds of materials you need for sales reps to pitch your products, services, or programs will vary. In turn, the more of these materials you already have prepared when recruiting your sales team, the more prospective reps will understand what they are selling. Later, the reps you hire can use these materials to become more familiar with what they will be pitching.

You can see the materials I used to recruit sales reps to pitch films, TV series, and documentaries at the AFM in the Appendix. Since the prospective reps were in different cities -- and even countries, I sent them a series of emails with PDFs of the sales materials they would use to rep my company. Initially, I had only one of these items prepared, but over the next two weeks as I talked to prospective reps, I developed four more PDFs of film projects to be pitched to distributors, sales agents, producers, and investors.

Organizing Your Sales Materials

If you have different audiences within your target market, you need different sales materials to reach them. For example, we created different flyers, so the reps could quickly explain the types of projects designed for different audiences (distributors and sales agents for completed films; producers for future projects) and give them the appropriate flyer or flyers with more details. These flyers also helped to explain to prospective reps what they would be doing at the AFM, so they could better decide if they wanted to be a rep.

Likewise, you can create the sales materials which the reps will use and show them these materials as part of the recruitment process. For example, if you have products, create flyers with illustrations. If you have services, create flyers or brochures which feature the benefits of using this service, and ideally include photos that show someone providing this service. For a program, the flyer can include illustrations and photos of the program being conducted. Additionally, show the rep any videos that he or she will be using to demonstrate what the product, service, or program does.

In the case of out of town prospects, you can send PDFs or JPGs by email or through a cloud-based storage program like Dropbox. For videos, you can post them on YouTube or embed them on your website and include links to them on the flyers. You can combine the information in multiple flyers in a single video, or you can put multiple flyers in a binder or folder with clear plastic envelopes to show in one-on-one meetings with prospects

Be ready to create additional sales materials if needed, such as if a prospect indicates that certain materials would be helpful in presenting your program. For example, maybe it would be helpful to have a detailed chart with product specs, a more complete description of what the service includes, or an outline of a typical workshop.

In sum, create and organize as much of your sales materials as you can to help you follow up after an initial inquiry from a prospective sales rep. In the interest of time, you may not have everything available when you start recruiting sales reps, so you may need to develop additional materials over the course of doing these interviews. Then, as the new materials are available forward them to the prospective reps who are still viable candidates, since these additional materials can help these prospects want to represent you.

Background Information about You and Your Company

Another key component of your sales materials for reps is a bio or informational sheet about you, your company and your track record. This background information is to not only convince prospective reps to represent you, but reps can show this to prospective customers, clients, and buyers, so they will want to buy from you.

Generally, this background information will be on a single page with a bio of about 150-300 words, and ideally a photo. If you are collaborating with another individual or company, include both of you on the same page and make the bio and photo smaller. A portrait is fine, or use a photo featuring you or your company providing a service or demonstrating a product.

In the text, highlight your most relevant achievements, note how long you have been in business, and other high points. An example of a one-sheet I used for the AFM is in the Appendix. It features my company and another company, since we were co-producing the films, documentaries, and TV series together.

CHAPTER 4: CREATING YOUR COMMISSION ARRANGEMENTS AND CONTRACTS

Besides showing prospective reps what they will do and supporting them with sales materials, whether for a specific event or ongoing arrangement, you need to clearly lay out what they will receive. This can take two forms:

- a description of what they will receive, which can be a single page, flyer or Word document.

- an agreement form that can be incorporated into a contract or an appendix to the contract that spells out the agreement terms in more detail.

I used both for the AFM program, and I've include copies in the Appendix.

There are a number of different payment arrangements, including commission only or draw plus commissions. Whatever arrangement you use, initially set this up so it is understood the person is working for you as an independent contractor. Otherwise, you will be subject to all kinds of employment law regulations and reporting requirements, which can be fine when you are more established and growing. But when you are first starting, an independent contractor arrangement it is more manageable.

A more detailed discussion about how to make sure your rep is considered an independent contractor and not an employee is in a future chapter. For now it generally will be clear the rep is not an employee if the rep is working for you on a short-term project, working part-time, is choosing his or her own hours, and is not under your direct control or supervision.

Payment Arrangements

There are several different payment arrangements. One that is almost never used with salespeople is the straight salary, unless someone is largely doing research for sales leads or administrating the gathering and distribution of leads to sales people. But for all practical purposes, when you have a small sales team, many reps will generate their own leads, while you or an assistant will provide them with leads, too.

The two payment arrangements, which you might realistically use are these:

- a small hourly draw against commissions
- a straight commission.

Offering a Draw and Commission

The hourly draw against commission is more common for large and medium-sized companies that have a team of sales reps who are representing only them. In that case, the reps are more like employees, who receive a small hourly payment designed to minimally support them. But they are expected to not only match that payment with sales but far exceed it so they receive a commission.

When you are just starting out, a draw and commission arrangement might work well if you are hiring sales reps for an ongoing arrangement, where you expect reps to bring in continued business for you. Then, that will affirm that they are expected to spend at least so much time, as agreed, working for you. If you do pay an hourly rate, ask for a report of what they owe do with what results, and keep the rate low and commission high enough, so they have an incentive to make sales. For example, you might pay $9-10 an hour as a draw against commissions, resulting in their being able to make much more. On the other hand, an hourly payment for sales is an expensive commitment to make. This payment might also attract prospective reps who are less aggressive in going after sales, because they have that base security. Then, too, the hourly payment may create an employment arrangement in that you are making regular payments, and you may be considered to exercise more control over an employee, since you are paying an hourly wage.

Offering a Straight Commission

A straight commission is the usual arrangement with independent reps, although you should have a high commission rate to make the no pay upfront offer appealing -- at least 25% or more typically 50-60%. Otherwise, you are likely to experience a high failure rate, since reps may find it doesn't pay to put much effort into representing you. In any case, when you do offer a straight commission, you may get fewer individuals interested in being a rep, but those who are interested will commonly be more aggressive in seeking out sales than reps with a draw, since they only get paid if a sale goes through. Still, this arrangement is a good test of a performance, since some independent reps will not be effective and you may have to terminate them. But at least you won't have a major financial commitment to pay someone who doesn't bring in any or only limited sales to you. Thus, for short term projects, I recommend that you offer a straight commission arrangement, which is what I did with the three reps I hired.

When you offer a straight commission, generally, an independent contractor can represent other companies, even competing companies in many cases. At least you have to offer the prospective rep that opportunity, even if the rep isn't representing anyone else at the time. This also means the rep can contact anyone they want and decide who they want to refer a prospective customer or client to, although they should keep you informed when they refer someone to you.

Just be sure the reps you hire are accurately representing you, whenever they do so. And if you provide a lead, they should only contact that party for you and not refer your lead to a competitor. In practice, you may have no control over exactly what the rep does, although ethically, they should present you, your company, and your products or services accurately and only talk to customers or clients about your company when you provide the lead. Should you find out that the rep is misusing your trust to give your lead information about other projects he or she is representing, you can end your relationship with the rep at any time.

Whatever your expectations, spell out your arrangements and what the rep will get in an agreement form. Your agreement should also clarify what reps can and can't do about dealing with other companies in your field with similar products or services. Specify if the reps have to have an exclusive arrangement for your type of product or service or not. Normally, you can't expect an exclusive arrangement, which many of the larger companies do with their reps, so they can't represent competing products, though they might have a separate business handling some other product or service. For example, some of the clothing and jewelry companies have a team of reps around the country who are using their name when they set up sales parties or do presentations to groups they belong to, such as a Chamber of Commerce or business referral group. But some reps also do other things, such as one rep who also had a pet walking business and another who led luxury tours.

On the other hand, some reps may be attracted to repping for you, because they already expect to attend a particular event or appeal to a similar target market for their own non-conflicting projects. Or maybe they want to learn about an industry, so they can enter it at a future date. For instance, some prospects interested in repping my films at the AFM were interested in contacting producers there, because they were interested in acting in their films or wanted to learn more about the industry in order to make contacts in the future. So making these connections weren't direct conflicts, and I agreed to have them rep us. But if they were pitching their own films, that would be a conflict and I wouldn't hire anyone who might push their films rather than ours, especially if we developed the lead.

Establishing a Commission for Different Types of Work

In establishing the commission, determine the going commission in your industry for what they will be doing. You should price your products and services in the range common in your industry, and factor in your costs and the commissions you will be paying on sales.

Some typical commission rates include these:

50-80% for selling a digital product

33-50% for selling a physical product

20-25% for setting up speaking engagements, workshops, or seminars

10% (or cost plus 10%) for referring work to a professional or tradesperson

10-15% for acting as an agent to sell a book or creative work

5% for finding money for a company.

If the rep is only providing a lead, rather than following-through to complete the sale or take the order, then he or she will typically get a share of that commission. For example, since I was getting a 5% finders fee for raising money for a film or finding a distributor, I agreed to give a percentage of my fee to reps who found leads for me, with that percentage based on what they did -- from simply collecting business cards (1%) to having an extended meeting with that contact (2 ½%). On the other hand, if the reps met with a lead with a writing project, they would split the standard 10% fee for film agents with me.

Whatever your commission, spell it out in a one-sheet, Word document, or PDF, and include the information or an appendix with this information in your agreement.

If you are still working out your system, it's fine to send prospective reps your description of commissions as a draft and invite their comments, which is what I did. After you get input from prospective reps, you can edit and refine the agreement. Such an approach can also contribute to prospective reps' buy-in, because they feel they are part of creating the arrangement. For example, you can send them the draft of the contract first smf get their agreement to it, or make any adaptations based on their comments if you find them helpful. Then, you can send them the completed commission arrangement and contract once you finalize them.

Examples of the commission arrangements and contracts we created for the AFM reps are in the Appendix.

CHAPTER 5: EXPLAINING THE REQUIREMENTS AND INTERVIEWING PROSPECTIVE REPS

Once prospective reps have responded to your ads, announcements, pitches at meetings, or referrals from contacts, the next step is interviewing those that initially seem qualified, to determine if there is a good fit on both sides.

Prequalifying Prospects

Once you have interested prospects, take some time to qualify them before you have an extended interview with them, especially if you have multiple candidates. Most importantly, check if they have had sales experience, and ideally, if they have worked as an independent sales rep before. If prospects aren't experienced in sales, look for people who have had experience dealing with the public, especially in a position of authority, or in persuasive capacity, such as being a teacher, minister, counselor, consultant, or trainer.

If you have to winnow down a large pool of applicants, prioritize them based who seems the most qualified candidates on a scale of 1 (high) to 10 (low).

Conduct an Interview

Interviews can take various forms, depending on whether the prospects are local or not and the amount of information they have provided in response to your initial pitch.

You might have an initial email exchange, where you explain a little more about the kind of rep you are looking for, your expectations, what the rep will be required to do, and the commission and payment arrangements. Or include much of this information in an initial interview.

Whether the follow-up interview is by email, phone, or face-to-face, you need to hear from the prospect about why he or she is interested in being a rep for you, his or her background in your field, and experience in selling.

If the prospect is still interested or wants more time to consider the opportunity, send the prospect a copy of the contract and any sales literature he or she hasn't already seen. If you have sent a fill-in-the blanks type of contract before, now send a contract where you have filled in the person's name. Fill in the commission payment based on the level of sales obtained (i.e. 1 1/2% up to

2500, based on a shared commission), and include your email. Add a date when the offer ends without a signed contract.

You can also conduct an interview if the prospect isn't quite ready but might be in the future.

Besides using this exchange or interview to determine if the prospect is still interested, you want to assess whether the prospect has the needed skills to represemt you effectively, will follow your guidelines, and accepts your commission arrangements.

Following are more details on this explanation and interview process.

Setting Up a Follow-Up Exchange or Interview

An email exchange can work well to provide the prospect with the sales material, draft of the contract, and details about what being a rep for you entails.

That's what I did after a prospect expressed interest in learning more. I sent more details on what the rep would do at the show, including speaking to leads I provided from emailing distributors and reps and contacting exhibitors at the show. I also provided files with one-sheets of our film projects, which the reps could use to briefly describe our current and future projects to distributors, sales agents, and investors. I also noted that the rep would need to have a pass for at least one day in order to get into the floors where the exhibitors had their rooms. I pointed out that the rep could set up meetings about their own projects, as long as they made the initial contact and were not following-up on a lead referred to them. Plus I explained that the rep would need to provide me with a report of everyone contacted and what happened, so I could follow up. Finally, I noted the other ways in which I would provide support to the rep, such as being available to answer any questions or talk to any contact who wanted more information than they could provide.

You can likewise conduct an interview, in which you explain what you expect the rep to do, what the return will be, and how you will help the rep in the field. Then, you can use an email to reaffirm in writing what you just explained, as well as provide a written summary of what you expect the rep to do. Also include a draft of the contract -- or a contract with the prospect's name and commission arrangement, if the prospect has already indicated an interest in going ahead with an agreement to rep you.

For example, when I spoke to prospects who expressed interest or called me for more information, I began by summarizing what going to the AFM as a rep would involve. Then, I asked the prospect to tell me about his or her experience and reasons for wanting to go to the AFM as a rep.

Creating Guidelines for Your Rep

Once you clarify what you want a rep to do, you can turn these explanations into written guidelines, which you can send in an email or in an interview, or do both, whatever works best for your style and that of the prospective rep.

If you are still developing these guidelines while you are interviewing and selecting the reps, that's fine. Just summarize the main activities the rep will engage in. Later, you can expand upon and finalize these arrangements as you prepare the materials the reps will need to represent you, which is what I did. As I sent out emails and conducted interviews on phone and in person, I gradually became clearer on what the reps would do. Then, I turned these preliminary plans into completed guidelines. Along the way, I submitted my evolving ideas to the prospective reps I decided to hire, so I turned their request for further details about what to do into guidelines on how to act in various situations.

You can see guidelines which I prepared for the reps, so they would know what to do and agree to do this in the Appendix.

Likewise, you can create a list of guidelines for what you want reps to do in representing you for a particular occasion, for a number of events, or for an ongoing arrangement. If they will be both representing you at a particular event and on an ongoing basis, create separate guidelines for different types of activities.

Go over the highlights of these guidelines with the prospective rep or with the reps you hire to be sure they know what to do when representing you and your company.

Following is a form you can use to think about what you want your reps to do. Then, give them a copy of this form, or copy it into a Word document or PDF to send to them by email or post in an online forum or shared document platform.

GUIDELINES FOR REPRESENTING _____ (NAME OF YOUR COMPANY) IN GENERAL

Following are guidelines for what to do and say in general when you are meeting someone to represent the company.

GUIDELINES FOR REPRESENTING _____ (NAME OF YOUR COMPANY) AT AN EVENT

Following are guidelines for what to do and say in general when you are meeting someone to represent the company.

Learning about the Prospect's Interests, Background, and Skills

It is critical to know about the prospect's motivations in being a rep, along with his or her past work, accomplishments, and skills. You can learn some of this in an email exchange, if the prospect can send you a resume, CV, or link to a website or Facebook page. It's also important to talk to the prospect in a phone or Skype interview -- and if the prospect is local, arrange to meet personally. As much as possible, work with local reps, since you can better assess them, and this one-on-one contact can help you in guiding and motivating them, and they may be more committed and dedicated as well.

However, if you are looking for reps for an event outside your area or have a business that lends itself to national clients and customers, many prospective reps will be outside your area. This was my experience in seeking reps to attend the 2017 American Film Market show in Santa Monica. Many prospects contacted me from two L.A.-based Meetup groups I took over after the organizers left, and one woman was acting in a film in Zurich before flying to the AFM. Thus, it was not possible to have personal meetings with these representatives, although I met with and hired a local rep I met at a local business networking group.

Prospective reps can provide you background information in various ways. My approach was to let people provide whatever they had available, since I was recruiting for a part-time commission-only job, where the sales reps would just make the initial contact and needed to know only basic information. So such a sales rep didn't have to have much past experience in outside sales, though that's a plus. Rather, they mainly needed to have an outgoing friendly persona, where I could follow-up with additional information to close the deal.

Likewise, be flexible in the type of background experience required and seek to hire the prospects who appear to have the best experience for being an independent sales rep in your industry, even though they are new to your field. As previously noted, prior outside sales experience is ideal, though other types of sales people and these dealing with people at work, such as teachers and counselors, can be well suited to being a rep. Having a detailed written resume to review is a plus, although sometimes this formal job experience will be less relevant doing outside sales work, since seeking such a position may be a new side activity for them.

For example, one rep who proved to be very successful for me was a physical therapist doing home-care for older adults. Yet she had an outgoing warm personality combined with good organizational skills that made her a great sales rep. It didn't matter that she didn't know much about the film industry, apart from enjoying seeing films. But on the plus side, she was very keen to enter the field, since she had some ideas for a documentary series about new ways to encourage healthier living for older adults.

Another rep was seeking a new career path and wasn't sure what he was doing. He had previously been in the financial field, which he left since he was bored with working with numbers. But a big plus was that he already lived in the L.A. area where almost everyone is involved in with films in some way, from acting and joining a crew to getting involved with financing. His goal was to gain more knowledge about the industry in order to eventually find a fulltime job or set up a private practice to help clients do deals. Additionally, one woman, who I also hired, called me from her film set in Switzerland. where she was a cast member. Once her part ended at the end of the month, she said she would be flying to L.A. and planned to attend the whole show. Inviting her to join the team seemed like the perfect choice at the time.

Key Questions to Ask in an Interview

However you get any background information, ask prospects some key questions and get answers that help to see if there is a good fit. For example, you want to be sure they are seriously interested, have the necessary skills to do outside sales, and have the time and availability when you need them. They also need to be willing to follow your guidelines on presenting your product or service and can follow-up with the necessary reporting information to you. Have a phone, Skype, or in-person interview, where you ask these key questions:
- Why do you want to be a rep for (YOUR PRODUCT, SERVICE, OR COMPANY?)
- What kind of experience have you had in this industry?
- What kind of experience have you had as a sales rep? (If they have had experience, what companies or what kind of companies did they work for?)
- What days and times do they want to work for you as a rep? (If this will be an ongoing project, how many hours do they want to work each week and on what days and times?)
- Have you reviewed the guidelines for what you will be doing? (Or if they haven't read them, you can tell them what these are no. But realize that not reviewing this material could be a warning flag, which shows that they are not serious, though they could be genuinely busy, so they didn't have time to review the guidelines before your interview).If they have reviewed the guidelines, are these guidelines okay for you? Is there anything you want to change?
- If you send a sample agreement form in advance, you can also ask: Have you reviewed the agreement? (Or if you haven't already sent this and they are still interested in being a rep, tell them you will send the agreement and send it

after your call. Then, have a follow-up call to determine if they are still interested, and if so ask them to sign the agreement and you will, too.)

- What do you do when you are not working?

If you can arrange an in-person interview, ideally arrange to meet at your office, since this is more convenient for you, and you have all your materials there. But if you both prefer, arrange this as a coffee, breakfast, or lunch meeting.

Besides asking the key questions in your interview, you might ask for references, especially if you hope this will be an ongoing relationship to rep you on a part-time basis over the next weeks or months. But if this is a short-term project where you hope to quickly put together a small team of reps to assist at a particular event, you may not have the time to check references. Or if only a few individuals are interested in being a rep, you may not want to delay hiring the reps and end up with no one representing you. In that case, I would recommend trusting your gut and taking a chance, if you have a commission-only arrangement, since you won't have any financial loss if things don't work out.

That's what I did, since I wanted a team of reps to represent me for a week. Besides, I had met one prospective rep at a local business networking group, and the other two responded to a mailing to one of my film industry Meetup groups. So I already felt a sense of connection and trust.

To guide your interview, write down the questions you plan to ask and use that as a guide. As the conversation goes along, you can add other questions to learn more or change the order as feels appropriate. You want to keep the interview conversational, so the prospective rep feels more comfortable and relaxed and so will respond to you more freely.

Take notes of the prospect's answers, and if this is a face-to-face interview, let the prospect know you will be taking notes to help you remember what you discussed.

Following is a guide you can use to write down the questions to ask. You can start with the suggested questions I used, and feel free to adapt them or add others relevant to your type of business. There is space for your notes, and you can increase the spacing or make your notes on a separate sheet of paper and attach those notes to your interview later.

INTERVIEW QUESTIONS TO ASK PROSPECTIVE REPS

NAME OF REP INTERVIEWED:

CONTACT INFORMATION:

Why do you want to be a rep for (YOUR PRODUCT, SERVICE, OR COMPANY?)

What kind of experience have you had in this industry?

What kind of experience have you had as a sales rep? (If you had experience, what companies or what kind of companies did you work for?)

What days and times are you available to work as a rep? (If this is an ongoing project: How many days, times, and hours do you want to work each week?)

Have you reviewed the guidelines for what you will be doing? (Or if they haven't read them, tell them: Here are the main things you will be doing. Then, explain them). Are these guidelines okay for you? Is there anything you want to change?

If you have sent this, have you reviewed the agreement? (Or if they haven't read it, tell them: I will send you a copy to review. In the meantime, here are the main points in the agreement. Then, explain them).

What do you do when you are not working?

(ADD IN ANY OTHER QUESTIONS YOU WANT TO ASK)

Is there anything you want to ask me?

Discovering other Possibilities

While you may only be interviewing to find reps for your team, you may find that you share interests with some of the people you interview. For example, they may have other marketing, social media, and writing skills you can use in your business. Or their interests and skills might open up opportunities for other types of collaboration. If you find such synergies, be open to exploring these possibilities if they are of mutual benefit.

For example, I had this experience when I met with one of the prospective reps. While she was a physical therapist working with an elderly population, she was especially interested in developing documentaries dealing with techniques for living longer and healthy aging. We began discussing this, since I had written a book on *The Science of Living Longer,* to be published the following month by ABC-Clio. The result was that we came up with an additional flyer about proposed documentaries on this topic to pitch at the AFM. And for these documentaries she was not only a sales rep, but a co-producer.

CHAPTER 6: HIRING REPS AS INDEPENDENT CONTRACTORS RATHER THAN EMPLOYEES

Since you are hiring reps on a part-time basis and often for a single short-term project, be sure to hire them as independent contractors and not as employees. Later, if the arrangement becomes more long-term or the work for you increases, setting up an employee relationship is fine. But when you are just starting out, an independent contractor arrangement is much simpler and less costly. Otherwise, if you hire an employee, you will be subject to a maze of employment laws, which include setting aside a percentage of each employee's payment for insurance and health benefits and filling out special tax forms for withholding tax. Plus the reps you hire will have to fill out forms and indicate that they have received wages from you on their tax forms.

As long as you comply with the guidelines that separate hiring independent contractors from hiring employees, you should be fine, and most prospective reps will prefer to be designated independent contractors, because you pay them everything up front rather than withholding some of their income for tax purposes.

If you have someone work for you as a part-time occasional sales rep on a long-term basis, include in your agreement with them that they understand that they are working for you as an independent contractor. Also, if they are receiving a commission, whether they are working on a commission-only or draw against commission basis, make it clear that any payment depends on a sale. And in some cases, this sale could involve some time for any payout, though it might later be substantial. For example, this was the case at the AFM, since an agreement with a distributor might mean no one earned any money until the film earned money after its release about a year late. Or often a script might be sold for no money or a minimum payment, even a symbolic $1, based on an option to buy if the film was produced, which could be a year or two later, when the producer raised enough money to produce the film. So while a sale could generate a lot of money in commissions in the future, there might be no quick payoff now.

The Difference Between an Independent Contractor and an Employee

You can find out the differences between an independent contractor and an employee if you Google "independent contractors employment law," "independent contractors employee," or "differences between independent contractors and employees." There are dozens of articles on the differences.

The IRS makes its own distinctions in pointing out the taxation requirements for both. As the IRS points out, "generally, you must withhold income taxes, withhold and pay Social Security and Medicare taxes, and pay unemployment tax on wages paid to an employee. You do not generally have to withhold or pay any taxes on payments to independent contractors."[1] So you can see why from a tax standpoint, it is better to have part-time occasional commission-only reps to be independent contractors, not employees.

A further distinction that the IRS makes is that an independent contractor is considered to be self-employed, though is not an independent contractor if he or she performs services that can be controlled by an employer about what will be done and how it will be done; the key is that the employer has "the legal right to control the details of how the services are performed."

However, if you are just providing guidelines on what to say and do, that is not providing complete control, since the rep can still set up his or her own appointments, adapt the guidelines to suit the occasion, and otherwise change the details of the performance."

One of the best articles: "Difference Between Independent Contractor and Employee" by Jean Murray, published October 6, 2017, describes the difference this way. "Employees are paid as salaried or hourly and may be subject to overtime. Employees are taxed on their income (they receive a W-2 form) showing their annual income), and you must also withhold federal and state income taxes and FICA taxes (Social Security and Medicare) from them. Your business must also make FICA tax payments)."[2] So again you can see why you don't want anyone you hire to be classified as an employee, because there's a whole lot of hassle and paperwork attached.

By contrast, to cite the Murray article again, "Basically, an independent business person who runs his or her own business but does work for another business (is an independent contractor)." Or an independent contractor could be an individual who has formally set up a business but is doing different projects for different employees on an occasional short-term or part-time basis.

The determination of whether the person you hire is considered an employee or independent contractor is based on three major factors:

- Behavioral Control, based on how much control you have over what the individual does. If a worker can set his or her own hours and works with little or no direction or training, he or she is probably an independent contractor, according to Murray, whereas if the employer trains and directs the work,

---

[1] https://www.irs.gov/businesses/small-businesses-self-employed/independent-contractor-self-employed-or-employee
[2] https://www.thebalance.com/independent-contractor-or-employee-what-s-the-difference-397912

including the hours of work, what tools or equipment should be used, specific tasks to be performed, and how the work is to be done, the worker is likely an employee.

- <u>Financial Control</u>, based on how you pay the worker and whether the worker can work for others at the same time. If you pay the worker a salary and restrict him or her from working from others, he or she is probably an employee; but if there is no salary, and the worker can work for others, he or she is more likely to be considered an independent contractor.

- <u>Type of Relationship</u>, based on whether the worker has benefits or not and whether the work is related to the company's core work. If there is a specific contract or the work is not directly related to the company's core work, he or she is probably an independent contractor.

Another article on LegalZoom, a website that provides individuals with all kinds of legal documents, points out some of the many characteristics that suggest someone is an independent contractor.[3] These include the following:

- The worker supplies his or her own equipment, materials and tools, or all the necessary materials are not supplied by the employer;

- The worker can be discharged at any time and can choose whether or not to come to work without fear of losing employment;

- The worker controls the hours of employment;

- The work is temporary rather than permanent;

- The work is not integral to the operations of the business.

- The worker does not gain a large proportion of their earnings from the business.

- The employer provides requests or an outline on how the worker does the work, but does not have authority over how the worker accomplishes the work.

In sum, this overview of the provisions distinguishing independent contractors and employees shows how hiring a team of independent sales reps meets the test for hiring independent contractors. For example, the reps will be using their own cars, computers, phones, and other items they own to meet with prospective customers or clients. They can set their own hours in setting up appointments. They are working for you on a temporary project or series of project. Their work is not integral to the business, since they are only working for you for a limited time, and you can readily hire someone else as a rep. Additionally, the person you hire is only getting a small percentage of their total income from you. And you are only providing guidelines, not specifying exactly on how you expect the rep to do the work.

---

[3] https://www.legalzoom.com/articles/employee-vs-independent-contractor-differences-you-need-to-know

Finally, a chart from FindLaw summarizes the differences between employees and independent contractors.[4] Following are the highlights from this chart.

[4] http://employment.findlaw.com/hiring-process/being-an-independent-contractor-vs-employee.html

Differences between Independent Contractors and Employees	
Independent Contractor	**Employee**
Generally provides consulting services to more than one company.	Usually works for only one employer.
Sets his or her own hours.	Works the hours set by the employer.
Works out of his or her own office or home.	Usually works at the employer's place of business.
Does not receive employment benefits from the employer.	Often receives employment benefits, such as health and disability insurance.
Works relatively independently.	Works under the control and direction of the employer.
Has the authority to decide how to go about accomplishing tasks, and does so without the employer's input.	Accomplishes tasks in the manner the employer has requested.
Incurs the costs associated with performing the job.	Tends not to incur costs and make investments in the work.
Has acquired very specialized skills and comes to the work relationship with a particularized education and experience background.	Has a general education and experience background, and receives special training from the employer in order to do the job better.
Is not subject to tax or FICA withholding, but pays his or her own self-employment tax.	Receives a net salary after employer has withheld income tax, Social Security and Medicare tax under the Federal Insurance Contributions Act.
Is not eligible for unemployment compensation benefits.	Wil likely to be eligible to receive unemployment compensation after layoff or termination.
Is not eligible for worker's compensation benefits	Will receive worker's compensation benefits for any workplace injury.
Generally (unless the consulting contract is for a specified term) can be let go by the employer for any reason, at any time.	Generally (unless employment is "at will") can be terminated by the employer only for good cause and with notice.
Is paid according to the terms of the contract, and does not receive additional compensation for overtime hours worked.	Is covered by federal and state wage and hour laws, such as minimum wage and overtime rules.
Usually is not protected by employment anti-discrimination and workplace safety laws.	Has the protection of workplace safety and employment anti-discrimination laws.
Is not entitled to join or form a union.	May be entitled to join or form a union.

As you can see from this chart and the previous discussion, you definitely don't want to hire your sales reps as employees, and based on the differences between the independent contractors and employees, you are not doing so. Aside from providing the sales reps with some general guidelines, you are not controlling what the sales rep does. You are not dictating the rep's hours, and he or she is working relatively independently with the authority to decide how to best obtain a sale of your product or service. He or she is deciding what hours to work and is working out of his or her own office or home – or is working out of a hotel or motel room or an associate's home or office while traveling. He or she is also paying any of the costs, such as for gas and meals, associated with working as a rep. And if your reps want to work overtime hours, that is their choice, and no additional compensation is due. In fact, if they are working on a commission basis, any payment is based on sales results, not on the time worked.

If you hire a sales rep to work on a part-time basis and pay them on an hourly basis a draw against commissions, you can set that up as an independent contractor arrangement, too. For example, if they work at home, they can report their hours. Or ask them to choose what hours to come in and leave. Let them decide on the best way to find any information they need to contact potential sales leads. And only check in from time to time to see how they are doing. Also, give them the freedom to choose what days they work andwhen they have to cancel working one day because of other priorities. For instance, I have a couple of people who have worked for me for several years for about 6-8 hours a week each, and they both set the days and hours when they will come in. If something comes up, they are free to reschedule for another day and time.

In sum, when you start out, it is best to hire reps as independent contractors, and if you follow the guidelines that distinguish independent contracts from employees, you are doing so.

Independent Contractor Agreement Forms

Having a separate formal independent contractor agreement may not be necessary when hiring a sales rep, since you can include that as part of an agreement to work on a particular project, as I did in hiring the AFM reps. But I have used them at times, such as when I hired someone to work on a database on a long-term basis.

If you feel more comfortable using an agreement to confirm that the person you hire is agreeable to working and being paid as an independent contractor, here's a form I have used in the past. Feel free to adapt it to your own arrangements with any rep you hire.

CHANGEMAKERS PUBLISHING AND WRITING

3527 Mt. Diablo Blvd., #273 . (925) 385-0608 . Fax : (925) 385-0880
changemakers@pacbell.net . www.changemakerspublishingandwriting.com

Date

INDEPENDENT CONTRACTOR AGREEMENT

It is understood that I am being hired as an independent contractor to (assist with various administrative tasks, such as formating books for sale on book websites, creating and updating databases, and posting copy on the social media/represent you and your company as a sales rep).

As an independent contractor, I understand I can choose my our own days and hours of work and I may be able to do some of the work at my own house.

It is understood that the payment will be at $____ an hour for the first month, and $____ an hour after that/on a commission only basis based on a percentage of sales as indicated on my agreement with you).

For _____   For (Your Name or Company Name)

_____   _____

Date : _____   Date : _____

PART II: WORKING WITH YOUR REPS

CHAPTER 7: CREATING THE DOCUMENTS YOU NEED TO WORK WITH YOUR REPS

Once you have hired a rep or small team of reps, you have to train them and coordinate what they do.

Having a Follow-Up Meeting to Go Over Guidelines on What to Do

While you can provide the reps with guidelines on what to do and say, you should also have a phone or online meeting with those out of town and a personal meeting with those in your area. This is a time to go over the highlights of any guidelines you have previously given them during the hiring phase or send this information to them now, so they can review it before your conversation. Highlight the most important points and check that they have received all of the documents you have previously sent them. Make sure they have all the documents they need for their presentations to potential clients, customers, and buyers, and if not send them any items they haven't received. If they are missing anything, email them attachments or give them the documents at your meeting. Give them some time to review everything they have, and arrange to talk again on the phone or online for a few minutes or resume your discussion at a one-on-one meeting.

Next, invite them to ask any questions. Answer if you can or let them know you will find out the answers, and after the meeting, do so. Sometimes reps will come up with a question you haven't thought of before, and if possible, tell them what you think is the best approach now. Otherwise, do some research or consider different scenarios and how the rep might respond. Then, write up some guidelines to indicate what to do if that situation comes up again.

For example, one AFM rep wanted to know what to do if an exhibitor's door was closed. Should they go and return when the door might be open. Another rep said she passed by a number of rooms with closed doors, because she didn't want to disturb the exhibitors, and later found that most of the doors were still closed. My suggestion for handling this situation: knock and if someone answers, try to set up an appointment with the person who handles acquisitions or get a card for the appropriate person to contact later. Later, the reps reported back that they were able to successfully set up appointments or get cards, since usually someone was in the room and opened the door.

In another case, a rep told me that one exhibitor had to cancel an appointment and only had available times when the rep had scheduled meetings or wouldn't be at the show. My recommendation was for me to assign the exhibitor to another rep, so that became a new policy I added to the guidelines: "If you can't arrange a convenient meeting with a distributor, sales agent or producer, refer this lead back to the sales team leader (in this case me), who will assign it to someone else. Or if you are in touch with other reps and one can handle the lead, reassign it to them, but advise the sales team leader who is now handling that lead."

In short, answer any questions you can at the time or come up with the answers by doing some research or thinking about what to do. Then. give the rep your answer. And if the question and answer is one that other reps might have, ask for their input, too.

Finally, remind the reps to keep you posted on what happens when they contact anyone, whether it leads to a sale or not. If possible, they should enter the information on a Contact Results sheet which you provide to them. Or they can write up the information in a document or email and send it to you. Then, you enter that information in the Contact Results sheet, so you can keep track of what the reps are doing with what results. Later, you can use that information to follow up and compensate the reps for their sales or leads, which result in you closing the sale. Sometimes reps may offer to give you information over the phone, but it is best not to do this, both to save you the time of writing down this information and because it is more accurate if the rep provides the information in writing.

In short, your initial follow-up interview after hiring the rep should cover the following:

1) Go over the highlights of the guidelines on what to say and do.

2) Provide the reps with any material they haven't received and give them some time to review this material, if any. Then, continue the discussion once they are familiar with the guidelines and information about your product, service, or company.

3) Ask for any questions, and answer them, or do some research, and provide the reps with the answers later by email, phone, or another one-on-one meeting.

4) Make sure that the reps have a Contact Results form and can fill out the form and send it to you or send you the needed information, and you fill it in.

Providing Business Cards and Credentials

At some point, you may want to provide your reps with business cards or formal credentials to show they are repping you. Initially, though, if the reps are representing you at a single short-term event, this may not be necessary. Instead,

60

the reps can use their own business cards. Then, you can explain they are reps for you when you follow-up on the information they provide.

For example, for the AFM, there wasn't time to get the reps business cards, since I made the final hiring arrangements just a few days before the AFM. Preferably, you should make these arrangements more quickly -- at least a week or two in advance. But in this case, the people who expressed interest and were good fits didn't know until four or five days before the event that they could go. Moreover, since they had to arrange to get badges for the event, they would have credentials from the show that could give them credibility at the event.

If you are going to provide the reps with business cards, a good way to start is with a company business card in which they can add their name. Then, you can continue to use the cards, if they don't continue to be a rep for you. If their relationship with the business continues, you can have cards printed just for them.

You will find many sources of business cards online or from local printers. The one I use is Vistaprint (www.vistaprint.com). You can get cards from them for about $10-30 plus shipping, depending on how many you order. And if Vistaprint is doing a promotion, these cards will be about 20-50% less. Sometimes the company will offer free cards, though their name and website is usually on the back, so I don't recommend that. Instead, pay for the cards, usually $10 more, so you get a plain white back, which I like, since contacts can make notes on the back of the cards. Alternatively, people are printing advertising pitches, lists of services, and tips for success on the back to encourage contacts to keep the cards and contact them.

Another approach to creating business cards is to provide postcard sized information on your company, along with a listing of your main products and services, and possibly a special offer with a promotional code.

Additionally, as previously noted, your reps can hand out a one-sheet or series of one-sheets to prospective clients or customers. You can send them the files so they can print out what they need. Or if you have a team of local reps, you can print out these flyers and postcards for them, based on the number of contacts they are likely to have. If they run out, they can print some more copies from the file.

If you or they have a color printer, that's great to print out the one-sheets in color, though color printing is substantially more expensive. Alternatively, print in black and white, but preferably print the flyers on colored paper. If you have multiple flyers, print each one on a different colored paper, so it's easy to tell them apart when you give them out or display them. The colored paper helps the flyers stand out, too, and it looks more professional than a series of different flyers on black and white.

Many trade shows and conferences have a table for sales literature, and if so, ask your reps to put some literature there. Preferably start with displaying about 25 copies, unless there will be a large a rep might want to have perhaps 25 copies unless there will be a large crowd; then put out more and replenish the display if needed. The reps should also expect to give out flyers to the people they meet with, though some contacts may prefer that the rep send them any flyers as an attachment, since they don't want to carry around these sales sheets at the show, although others may prefer to include the flyer with their handouts from attendees at the show. Generally, if there is no display table, about 10 to 15 print-outs of each handout to start with is fine. Then, the rep can print more if needed, though generally this amount should be enough for one day.

It is also best to make any print-outs before going to an event. Though some hotels and convention centers have a printer or print-center for guests, many do not. Or sometimes a printer may not work. As a result, it's best not to wait until the show, as one of my reps did, only to find that the printer was out of service, so she had nothing to hand out, which contributed to her not doing very well after several meetings.

Getting Reports from Your Reps

Keep track of what your reps are doing with what results, so you know how well they are representing you. To this end, ask them to give you daily reports of who they contacted and what happened. In some cases, they may be in a position to write up an order, close a sale, take an application, or obtain credit card information to charge a purchase, advance payments for a service, or a retainer for a future product or service. In other cases, they will provide information, so you can follow up to provide the contact with more information, negotiate, or close the sale.

Whatever the situation, you should have explained what to do, and if a rep still is unsure or needs additional information, provide that now. You want to be sure your reps are fully prepared. Also, advise them that you will be available for any questions by email, online, or phone. If your schedule permits, be available to talk to any contact to answer they are meeting with to answer any questions the prospective client or customer might have. You can also use this call to reassure a wavering contact that your company is real, knowledgeable, and ready to respond to any client or customer concerns.

Creating Reporting Documents for Your Reps

To help your reps provide you with the needed reporting information, give them a reporting document to enter this information or ask them to give you a list with this information so you can insert it in the document. They should also add their notes about what happened at the meeting, their impressions of the contact, and how to follow up, so they or you can contact the lead, depending on your arrangements with the rep.

For instance, I asked the reps at the AFM to present our film projects that were available now or in the near future, and I planned to follow-up from there. I used this approach, since these reps had a great outgoing personality for making the initial contacts. But they didn't know much about the industry beyond the descriptions on the one-sheets. So they didn't have the necessary knowledge they needed to follow through and close a deal. Thus, they only had to report the results of their initial meeting, and then I would follow up with their contacts and provide more information about distributing, agenting, producing, co-producing, or investing in our films. I used the reporting information they sent me to know what the contacts were interested in, so I could respond accordingly.

In addition, have a form to keep track of the appointments of each of your reps, indicating who they are meeting with at what time and where. This information is especially critical if you have two or more reps and you are setting up some of their meetings, so you know when they have time available to set up other meetings for them. Or, if possible, find a time when all of the reps are free so they can meet together, or with a prospective client, customer, or others. Having this scheduling information was especially important at the AFM when I had to find a time when everyone was available, so they could meet with one of the two film directors and producers. After some juggling, I found a time when they could meet, and I scheduled the meeting for everyone.

How to Create these Documents

You can create reporting forms in various formats. One way is to create a Word documents with tables or set up an Excel spread sheet. Then, fill it in with the indicated information and provide these to your reps in files they can print out. Another approach is to set up the forms online, such as in a Google doc. Or use other online spreadsheets. Plus ask your reps to send you more detailed notes in a separate document.

Whatever format they use, they should pull out the major things you should know to follow up, rather than sending you raw files with all of their exchanges with you and prospective clients or customers.

For example, as an example of what not to do, one rep sent me a file from her phone that included every exchange. When I opened it to print it out, it was a document of 215 pages. So I wrote her back and told her to give me the major results of these conversations, not the whole file, and eventually she did send back a list with the highlights of her meetings with interested contacts..

Following are examples of the two types of forms you can use:

- a Scheduling Form to keep track of what everyone is doing, so you can set up meetings for them;

- a Contact Reports Form, which each rep uses to indicate who they met with what results, or you can fill in the form with information from the rep.

As noted, you can create these forms in a Word document, Excel file, or other document and send them to the reps as an attachment or post them online. This way, you or the reps can enter the information there and everyone can see what everyone else is doing, unless you create restrictions about who can see what.

Scheduling Form

To make a simple scheduling form, create an Excel file with the purpose of the form on top (ie: Meetings at the AFM), an indication of how you are breaking down the schedule (ie: Date and Name of Sales Rep), and include the time of the meetings header at the top left. List all of the times when meetings will be scheduled, based on the time between meetings (ie: 15 minutes, 20 minutes, 30 minutes), and create a record for each time. Also, include the name of the rep for each date. Should the reps be available on different dates, indicate this on the schedule, by listing the available reps for each date.

Here's the chart I used for the AFM. The times beginning at 9:00 a.m. are divided by 15 minute intervals -- 9:15; 9:30; 9:45, and so on, and across the top on the next row, I indicated the rep who will be there on each date. The chart illustrates the scheduling through noon, though the chart goes through 6 p.m. each day. You fill in each meeting as the rep sets them up. Or if the chart is online, whoever sets up the meetings -- you or the rep -- can fill in this information there.

Time	Thurs. Nov. 2	Fri. Nov 3		Sat. Nov. 4		Sun. Nov. 5		Mon. Nov. 6		Tues. Nov. 7	
	Charmane	Charmane	Linda	Charmane	Brett	Linda	Charmane	Linda	Charmane	Charmane	Brett
9:00											
9:15											
9:30											
9:45											
10:00											
10:15								Sadie Hopkins Films			
10:30		Randate Roland Nolan						Sadie Hopkins Raghav Pern			
10:45											
11:00						TBA Studios Tim Vetabol					
11:15											
11:30								Media Luna Floriano Buonix			
11:45											
12:00						Dickie Bruse Richard Yeagley					
12:15											
12:30											
12:45											

Meetings at AFM by Changemakers Productions Team — Date and Team Members at AFM

This regular updating can help you avoid double booking, if you are scheduling some of the appointments for the rep and the rep advises you upon getting each booking, so you can update the chart, or you or the rep can add this information to an online chart. If only the rep is setting up the meetings, less frequent updates are fine.

Having this information is also useful when you set up a meeting with two or more of the reps and another party, such as when I set up a meeting between the three reps and one of the producers/directors for the films they were repping.

Contact Results Form

Following is an example of a Contact Results form, which is labeled according to the particular activity or event it is used for -- in this case, for AFM Contacts at the American Film Mart show. This is a copy of the Excel sheet, though you can create this form in a Word doc or online spreadsheet.

While I have set this up as a spreadsheet, you can also create a form where you list each item in order and put each listing on a page in a Word doc. You can list whatever items are most relevant for the rep to include after each meeting, and the rep can provide the rest of the information on a notes page.

For example, the information I asked the reps to collect included the following:
- Company Name
- Type of Company (ie: Distributor, Sales Rep, Producer)
- Name of Contact
- Title
- Email

- Phone
- Referral Name (if there was another person to contact about acquisitions)
- Title of Referral
- Email of Referral
- Phone of Referral
- Areas of Interest
- Comments for Follow-Up

AFM Contacts - Name of AFM Rep:

Company Name Type/Website	Name	Title	Email	Phone	Referral Name	Title	Email	Phone	Areas of Interest Comments for Follow-Up

Having the information in this compact way provides an overview of everyone the rep met with and what happened, so you can more easily follow through. The chart also helps you know the rep's contribution to any sale or agreement made after you follow up, so you can compensate the rep accordingly.

For example, for the AFM, my contract with each rep stated that they would receive a share of my finder's fee of 5% in finding distributors or sales agents for our completed films or a share of an agent's commission of 10% in finding producers, production companies, or investors for scripts or the films to be developed. This percentage would range from 20% to 50% of my fee, depending on what they did -- from getting a name or business card of a person for me to contact (20%) to finding the contact and having a meeting with them (50%). The reps understood that, any earnings from these contacts might be uncertain and unpredictable, because that is the nature of the film industry. While a film could be picked up by a network or cable producer with a high upfront payment of about $250,000 to $500,000, it might not receive any earnings from a distributor, until the film earned out enough to cover the distributor's marketing fee in distributing the film through numerous venues, from DVD sales to theatrical showings and streaming. But the reps still were game do this, since they were interested in learning about the film industry and hoped to be part of these or future film projects. Thus, while any earnings might be uncertain, the chart indicated what these percentages would be in calculating any future earnings.

Additional Notes Page

Finally, you can get the rep's notes on contacts of prospective clients and customers in one of two ways.

1) The rep sends you a description of what happened with each contact. Then, you attach the notes to the Contact Form, and refer to it as needed, when you follow up or have any questions to ask the rep about the meeting.

2) You use a formal Notes page, which the rep uses for additional information after meeting with a particular client or customer. n example of such a Notes page is on the following page. Feel free to adapt it to your own product or service.

NOTES ON MEETINGS WITH PROSPECTS		
Date of Meeting	Name of Contact Company, Email, and Phone Number	Notes on What Happened, Interests of Prospect, and Follow-Up Needed

CHAPTER 8: COORDINATING YOUR SALES TEAM

Now that you've hired and oriented your team, the next step is coordinating what your team members are doing in the field. There are several ways to do this. Determine what works for you.

- Leave it up to the reps to find their own leads wherever they want.
- Assign the reps certain territories, days, and times to find their own leads.
- Create a more centralized system for assigning leads to reps, based on when and where the prospect is or wants to meet; or rotate assignments from one rep to another.
- Combine a system for assigning leads and letting the reps find their own leads.
- Vary your approach for different projects.

Letting Reps Find Their Own Leads Wherever They Want

Letting reps find their own leads wherever they want is the "open season" approach. Reps can choose their own time and place to make contacts, though they get their guidance, training, and materials from a central source. I've mostly run into this approach with multi-level companies that have an organized hierarchical system based on sponsorships. They have a "survival of the fittest" or "whoever gets there first" approach, where the "the early bird gets the worm." This approach works well for certain types of businesses, and it breeds a mix of competition and cooperation between sales reps in the organization, who sometimes form teams to work together and put on the opportunity meetings, where they bring prospects and sometimes split up leads that come from joint mailings and other efforts.

I have also seen this approach work well on a local level, where a representative for a land banking company looked for finders to refer prospects to her and gave them a small percentage of her commission. She offered 2% just for sharing the lead, and finders could contact prospects anywhere, after going through a few hours of training by watching videos, meeting with a local team leader, and checking in every week or two about their progress in finding leads. Given that land investments to acquire a piece of property began at $25,000, this 2% could result in substantial earnings, just for making a few phone calls or sending out a few emails, since finders were not supposed to do any selling. They were just supposed to make an introduction to the program by referring prospects to a brief video with a few key points about the program. Then, the rep for the program would do the rest.

I even participated as one of these finders for a while by sending out an email to thousands of real estate agents in California would work. But this approach didn't work, since a cold call emailing about making a $25,000 plus investment in undeveloped land could readily seem like a scam, and most real estate agents don't make huge incomes, and they are trying to sell their clients on a particular home or other piece of real estate they are representing. Yet a few other people who met personally with people in the real estate field, such as a speaker and trainer who gave motivational programs to real estate agents, did well.

However, a major disadvantage of this approach of having reps find all their own leads is that you can hire a number of reps who go off on their own but they aren't very committed to the program. They might sign up to be sales rep but don't do very much, and you lose track of what they are doing, if anything. Thus, when you are starting out to build your first sales team, I don't recommend leaving it totally up to reps to find their own leads. You want a committed team of reps you can work with and help them become successful; then, if they are successful, you can use their success to recruit others in the future when you do have the luxury of adding a mix of very enthusiastic, dynamic sales reps and others who may or may not do anything. But initially, you want a small committed team you can work with closely to help them succeed.

Assigning the Reps Certain Territories, Days, and Times to Find Their Own Leads

Assigning reps certain locations or times is a variation on the "open season" approach, except that you are limiting where and when the sales rep can find potential contacts. This approach can help to cut down group conflict and competition over who gets credit for the sale, since reps have different assignments. But they still have to find the leads or follow up on leads that come to them from a central location based on their territory or shift.

In this case, since the reps have different territories, coordinators tend to exercise more control over what the reps are doing to make sure they are performing well. After all, assigning one person to a territory or shift means that someone else who might be more successful can't handle that location.

Often this approach is used by larger companies. For example, at business referral groups I have met sales reps for Paychex, a company involved with payroll and other human resources management issues, and each rep is assigned a certain city or county area, and if they encounter someone from another area at any of these meetings, they refer the lead to the rep who handles that territory.

Other companies that use this assignment approach have different sales reps taking the calls at a central location or call center at certain times. Or reps in a central area, such as an auto sales company, alternate who takes what phone call or lead.

Creating a More Centralized System

Another approach, which I mostly used with AFM reps, is creating a centralized system, where you coordinate and assign leads to reps, so they can set up meetings based on their own schedule.

Sometimes it works well for you to manage the master schedule, so you set up appointments for the reps and provide them with the details of who they are meeting with where and when. Then, any changes in the scheduling are made through this master system. This is the approach of some large companies, such as the Geek Squad, which handles all calls for service through a central call center, when you call for either an in-store appointment or home visit by a tech. A call center rep makes the arrangements, including sending out confirmation emails for the appointment. Everything is managed centrally from an 800 number, and the central office sends out follow-up emails to confirm the appointment, make any changes, and get feedback on how everything went. Some local businesses similarly use such a system to set up appointments for their owners, employees, or sales people.

Likewise, you can use a more centralized system if you want more control in finding leads, passing them on to your reps, and working out their appointments, based on when they and the prospect are available.

However, it can take a lot of effort to coordinate everything centrally, even with only a few reps. You not only have to keep track of everyone's schedules, but you have to match each rep to a time a prospect prefers and set up the arrangements for the location, day, and time of the meeting. Then, if there are changes, which may often occur, you have to make those scheduling changes and let the sales rep know that the prospect wants to make that change. And if the sales rep is running late, he or she has to tell you, and you have to communicate that to the prospect, unless you arrange for the sales rep and prospect to communicate themselves about the forthcoming appointment.

Unless you are a super-detailed person who likes dealing with all of those logistics, this centralized coordination of everything can become a nightmare. So I don't recommend it, and I never tried it or wanted to try it myself. Instead, what I found worked best was creating a centralized system for obtaining many of the leads and then assigning these leads to the reps, based on when they were available for meetings. Additionally I left most of the details to the sales rep, who could communicate directly with the prospect to set up appointments, manage any changes, have a meeting, and report back to me on the results.

Sending Out an Initial Mailing to Get Leads

I got the initial leads by doing mailings to the AFM exhibitors, who were mostly distributors and sales agents, and to attendees, who were mostly buyers of films, producers seeking distributors and sales agents, and filmmakers hoping to make industry connections. In these mailings, I sought to set up meetings for our reps with distributors and sales agents for completed films and with attendees for future projects.

You can see examples of the letters I sent out in the Appendix. Similarly, to set up meetings for your own reps, you can send a letter where you describe the product or service you are offering and how you would like to set up a meeting with your rep to discuss this. While my letters were directed to setting up a meeting for a particular show, you can send out a letter at any time to set up such a meeting. Then, the recipients reply to you, and you can either refer them to a particular rep or schedule the meeting for the rep, and let the rep handle arrangements from there.

Following Through to Finalize Any Deals

After the reps had meetings with interested prospects, I followed through to negotiate and finalize any deals. The only time I got involved in these communications to set up or change appointments was if a rep couldn't handle a changed appointment or had an emergency, so he or she couldn't handle the appointments that day. Then, I change the arrangements with a prospect from one rep to another rep, who was available on that day and time. The new rep took over and communicated directly with the prospect, much as the first one did. If there was no rep to have a meeting, I talked to the prospect myself by phone and sent any documents as email attachments. After that, if the prospect was still interested, I followed up just as I would if the sales rep had met with the prospect and referred him or her to me for follow-up.

Keeping Track of Meetings for Your Reps

Whether or not you or your reps are scheduling the meetings with your leads, keep track of who is meeting with who for your records and to schedule additional meetings as needed between your reps and you, with each other, or with prospects. You can use a chart to keep track of the meetings or use the emails of meetings the reps send you, if you haven't yet entered them in the master chart. That's what I did for the AFM.

Here's an example of how I began scheduling these meetings for the reps who were at the show on different days. This chart illustrates the first few entries.

	Time	Thurs. Nov. 2 Charmane	Fri. Nov 3 Charmane	Linda	Meetings at AFM by Changemakers Productions Team — Date and Team Members at AFM					
					Sat. Nov. 4 Charmane	Brett	Sun. Nov. 5 Linda	Charmane	Mon. Nov. 6 Linda	Charmane
5	9:00									
6	9:15									
7	9:30									
8	9:45									
9	10:00									
10	10:15								Sadie Hopkins Films Sadie Hopkins	
11	10:30		Bidslate Roland Rojas						Raghav Peri	
12	10:45									
13	11:00					TBA Studios Tito Velasco				
14	11:15									
15	11:30								Media Luna Floriano Buono	
16	11:45									
17	12:00					Dickie Bruce Richard Yeagley				
18	12:15									
19	12:30									
20	12:45									

As I got reports from the sales reps indicating when they had scheduled meetings, I entered them by day and time into the chart. When I initially only had reports from two reps, I compared their reports side by side for different days to determine the times they still had available for setting up meetings, though mostly they set their own schedules.

For example, here are the reports of two of the reps.

73

Combining a System for Assigning Leads and Reps Finding Leads

Still another approach for handling leads is to combine sending leads to reps with assigning territories where reps can find their own leads or let the reps find their leads anywhere.

While I mostly used the centralized system approach by giving reps the leads I obtained from sending emails to exhibitors and attendees, I also assigned the reps different floors on which to contact exhibitors. For instance, since I had three reps at the show and the exhibitors were spread out fairly evenly over six floors, I assigned each rep two floors -- 3 and 4 for one rep, 5 and 6 for another, and 7 and 8 for a third. The result was about 50 leads for each rep, plus I gave them a list of 20 exhibitors not to contact, since the film producers/directors were already meeting with them.

At the same time, the sales reps were free to contact whoever they wanted in other areas of the hotel where exhibitors and attendees gathered -- a pool area limited to those with badges for the day or the whole show and a lobby area, open to anyone. Additionally, if the reps went to any of the nearby coffee shops and lounges where show participants gathered, they were welcome to approach anyone.

In the event a rep approached a prospect who was already contacted by another rep, then it was back to the "open season" approach of whoever made that connection first. Otherwise, the reps were limited to their assigned territories or to the leads I forwarded to them based on the days and times they were available.

Varying Your Approach for Different Projects

Finally, consider using different approaches for handling leads for different projects. While this combined approach worked for the AFM, since the reps had different ways of contacting prospects -- from following up on my leads to looking for leads in assigned territories or other areas, sometimes it might be better to use one approach rather than another.

For example, if you can't provide leads yourself, let the reps develop the leads however they want. If the reps are in different areas, divide up the areas based on where they live. Or if the reps are setting meetings on different days, you can refer leads to them based on when prospects want to set up a meeting.

While I used emails to prospects from a mailing list I developed, another approach to developing leads is using your website as a clearinghouse. To do so, you might post notices or ads on various platforms, such as Google, Facebook, or YouTube, and refer people to your website. Then, when people sign up, refer them to different reps. Or you might use your website as a platform where the reps can pick up leads on different days or alternating which leads they take. Or perhaps the reps can split up the leads based on where the prospect lives.

In short, there are many ways of developing and coordinating leads, whether you develop them or your reps do. But whatever system you use, you or your reps have to follow up to close the deal. In some cases, your reps can take orders, such as if they are pitching a simple product or service. In other cases, they are acting as door openers, and you have to follow up to provide prospects with the details to participate, such as for an expensive or complicated product, service, or program, like distributing a film, investing in land banking, or signing up for an in-depth course, coaching, or mastermind program. Consider the different approaches for working with reps yourself and decide what works best for you.

CHAPTER 9: DEALING WITH REPS WHO DON'T WORK OUT

From time to time it happens. You bring a rep onto the team thinking of great possibilities, but they don't perform or engage in a series of gaffes that show they can't do the job. They make all kinds of promises, but don't deliver. What do you do?

An Example of a Rep that Washed Out

I had this experience with one of the three reps I hired for the AFM, and I had to turn her responsibilities over to other reps or handle the follow-up myself.

The arrangement started with such high hopes. I sent out an announcement to my film Meetup groups in the Bay Area and LA., and -- let's call her Andrea -- responded. She told me she was now filming in Europe, but after the filming wrapped on October 30th, she would fly back to L.A. and arrive on November 1st. Then she expected to go to the whole AFM from the 2nd to the 8th. She explained that she hoped to meet with producers about future acting gigs, and she would be delighted to represent Changemakers Productions in meeting with distributors, sales agents, and producers, because she wanted to learn more about the film industry.

It seemed like the perfect arrangement, since one other rep would be at the show on the 4th, 5th, and 6th, and another on the 4th and 7th. So she could take meetings on the 2nd, 3rd, and 8th, meet with everyone on the 4th, and handle any meetings the others couldn't go to on other days. Plus it would be easier on everyone to split up the six floors between three people rather than two.

Thus, everything seemed to be set for the AFM, and I emailed Andrea the files with an agreement to sign, guidelines for what to do, and flyers she could print out.

But in hindsight, the first warning sign occurred when Andrea didn't email or call me after she arrived on the 1st. However, I was able to assign interested prospects to the other reps, so her delayed call didn't seem a problem at the time.

Then, though I did hear from her on the afternoon of the 2nd, I continued to act as if everything was fine, so I forwarded emails to her from five prospects, and she contacted them to set up appointments. But she didn't let me know who she was going to see, though the other reps did this. Still, I hoped for the best.

However, late that night, Andrea emailed me to say she had hurt her foot, so she had to go to the doctor the next day and couldn't meet with the appointments she had made for the 3rd. Instead, she sent a list with some first names and a few emails to contact them, so I had to do some research in my original emails to track down the contact information, though one name remained a mystery. Then, when I emailed Andrea and asked her to call me or give me her phone number, so I could call her, she explained that she had a European phone and couldn't make any calls in the states.

Thus, we could only email each other. Later, when I told her in an email about the meeting of all the reps with the directors/producers the next day, she didn't show, though she emailed me that night to say she had gone to the AFM party and had gotten a lot of business cards that day. But when I asked about getting the names on the cards so I could follow up, she never sent them. Then, when I reminded her in an email that she would need to get a badge to see the exhibitors on the 5th and 6th floors assigned to her and asked again about getting the names of the people she contacted, she never got back to me about that, so I could only presume that she didn't get a badge. Her only email a day later was an apology that she wasn't able to meet with the people on the 3rd.

Needless to say, this was clearly a rep who didn't work out, and after our last exchange, I sent any further leads from my emails to exhibitors and attendees to the other two reps. I also split up her floor assignments between them. At least the event was very successful with those two reps, and I never heard anything from Andrea again.

What to Do If a Rep Isn't Working Out

This experience with Andrea, plus additional work I have done in conflict resolution and writing books on this subject, helped me come up some of the following key suggestions of what to do if a rep isn't working out.

You Can't Always Tell in the Beginning

Sometimes when you first hire someone, it can be hard to notice any warning signs of potential problems. Someone might give you all the right answers to convince you he or she is interested in working for you for the right reasons. So it can be hard to tell.

For example, Andrea came from one of my film industry Meetup groups, indicated she wanted to learn more about the industry, was already acting in an independent film, and planned to attend the entire AFM. She understood she would need a ticket to meet the exhibitors, and she indicated she planned to get one. Perhaps I could have additionally asked for some references and contacted them. But I had limited time to assemble a small team, and since this was for a commission-only sales position, I needed to bring aboard people who wanted to get to know the film industry and make connections for themselves, as well as for my film projects. So, looking back, Andrea seemed to have the necessary interest and enthusiasm to do a great job.

Likewise, if you are in a situation where you want to put together a small sales team quickly, especially if this is for an upcoming event and you are only paying a commission, you might need to similarly decide on who seems to be the best fit based on your initial impression and what they tell you. So you have to make a hiring decision based on what you know at the time. You may not always be right, but under the circumstances, you made the best choice you could. So don't have any recriminations for making a misjudgment.

Another reason for no regrets is that your decision was fine at the time, but later some unexpected circumstances interfered with the rep's ability to do the work, because sometimes, as they say: "S**t happens!" Unexpected emergencies occur. These external incidents can affect anyone. So that could be a reason why your initial hiring choice didn't work out

Thus, whatever led you to choose as you did in the beginning, if problems develop later, don't have recriminations, don't engage in self-blame. Simply see what there is to learn from the experience and move on.

Look for Any Signs of Potential Problems Early On

Be ready to notice and respond to any signs that the rep may not be performing as expected. Sometimes it can be easy not to notice or to dismiss these initial signs of possible problems, but be alert to catch them early.

For example, in my case, the first warning sign was Andrea's delay in contacting me when she first landed. She didn't call me until the second afternoon after she arrived, which I should have taken as a sign that she wasn't as committed to being a rep for my company as she led me to believe with her initial enthusiasm and seeming understanding of what to do. Also, I let it slide when she said she hadn't yet downloaded the documents I sent and didn't understand that I wouldn't be giving her copies myself, since I wasn't at the show. And while she acknowledged my suggestion that there might be copiers at the hotel with a quick "Okay," she did not affirm that she would make copies to give to interested contacts. In retrospect, I realized that I was trying too hard to be nice and understanding, rather than going over any expectations for being a rep and getting her to reaffirm that she had the documents I sent, understood what to do, and agreed to the arrangements. Plus, I didn't get her signed agreement, whereas the other reps wanted to be sure they had signed the contacts with me.

Thus, it's important to pay attention to how and when a rep responds, and if the rep delays or seems uncertain about what to do, let the rep know upfront about anything the rep has done that does not meet your expectations or protocol. For example, I should have asked Andrea why she didn't call me right away, and I should have gone over my expectations for what the reps should do, which included keeping me informed regularly by phone or email about who they were meeting with. In this case, had I asked these questions and reaffirmed my expectations, I would have learned that Andrea didn't call right away because she couldn't use her phone from Europe to make calls in the U.S. and had to wait to use a pay phone, such as at the AFM, in order to call me. In turn, this information would have helped me recognize her big disadvantage in being only able to send emails or use pay phones at the AFM, making it difficult for her to set up meetings or change schedules.

As Soon As You See Any Potential Problems, Say Something

Once you notice any potential problems, say something to that rep as quickly as possible. Then you can reaffirm what the rep is supposed to do and make sure he or she can meet these expectations under two scenarios:
- If the rep already understands the requirements from your initial email exchanges and communications, this review should reaffirm what you are doing. It also should show the rep that you expect professionalism in your rep and also show the rep that you expect professionalism in your rep.
- If the rep hasn't signed the agreement or read over the guidelines about what you expect of the reps, this is another sign that this rep isn't right for you, particularly since the agreement outlines the commission they will get for any closed sales of film projects. And who wouldn't want a signed agreement about when they might get paid?
The advantage of saying something at this point is you can get the agreement for repping you back on track, if it is starting to go off the rails. Or if everything still fine, let the rep know you want to help and to ask you any questions. Or perhaps more firmly state what you expect and indicate that you will check up on what the rep is doing from time to time to make sure he or she doing what's expected.
If the rep doesn't agree to do what is expected, the solution is easy. Tell the rep that you don't think things are working out and explain why. Should the rep respond by saying that he or she really wants to do this assignment, perhaps relent and ask the rep to follow up on a few referrals from you and see how he or she does. If it's a good job, he or she is back on the team; or if not, that's the way things go, and it's better to cut your losses early on, rather than after the rep has disappointed you in other ways.

Find a Replacement or Assign What the Rep Was Supposed to Do to Others

If you decide a rep isn't working out, if possible, bring in someone else to take over that role. Maybe a previous candidate you turned down might work out now. Or maybe you might do some quick local advertising, if you can bring the new rep up to speed in a short time.

But if you can't find a replacement soon enough, as was my experience at the AFM, assign what the rep was supposed to do to other reps by splitting the work between them. Tell them what happened and why, and ideally, they will have the time and ability to take on this additional work. If so, give them the information you previously gave the rep they are replacing, so they can take over the assignment as easily as possible.

Giving them some advance notice also helps, if you suspect that a rep isn't working out so they can prepare to take on this additional work if necessary. Explain why you think they can readily handle the additional work, such as noting your past experience in doing this work yourself.

I had to do such juggling of assignments when Andrea bailed on being a rep. For about a day I was uncertain whether she could continue, when she told me she had to go to the doctor and sent me a list of appointments which she couldn't make on the first day of being a rep. So I wrote to the six individuals on that list to find out the other days they were available, and then I referred them to one of the other reps who would be there that day. At the same time, I advised the reps that I wasn't sure if Andrea could continue because of her injured foot, so I might need them to contact exhibitors on the floors originally assigned to her by taking one additional floor each. I also described my experience in going to the AFM several years earlier, and I explained how I had contacted exhibitors for a few minutes each by going up and down the halls and making a brief introduction to my company or learning who to contact about acquisitions in the future. So it might take the reps about an hour to cover the extra floor. In turn, both reps said they could handle the extra assignment if necessary.

The following day, when Andrea told me she couldn't use her phone from Europe in the U.S. and didn't have a badge to get onto the floors with exhibitors, I told the other two reps what happened, and they each took one of the floors. Plus now I referred any new contacts to them to set up meetings on the days they were at the show, or I followed up myself. Thus, in the end, the two reps, with a little extra support from me, were able to take over the work the rep couldn't do.

Likewise, you can often do the same when someone can't do the work for whatever reason. Reassign the work to other reps if they are available to handle it, or do some or all of the additional work yourself.

Indicate that the Arrangement to Be a Rep Is Terminated

A final step is to make sure the rep knows when any arrangement to rep you is terminated.

Sometimes you don't need any formal legal termination statement, such as when the rep has not signed an agreement to rep you, is working on a commission only basis, and is a no show. Then, an exchange of emails indicating that this relationship has come to an end is sufficient.

For example, Andrea never signed the agreement to be a rep at the AFM, never met with anyone I referred to her, did not send me any contact information for anyone she met on her own, and could not meet with any exhibitors, because she didn't get a badge to be able to go to the hotel rooms. Thus, after she sent me an email apologizing because she couldn't meet the individuals I referred to her and later emailed me to say she was sorry about all the trouble she caused by having to cancel her appointments and did not get a pass for the AFM, that was enough to show the rep relationship was over. So I simply sent her a brief email saying I was sorry things didn't work out, and that was that.

In other cases, if you have a signed no commission agreement but the rep has not done anything to earn a commission and you no longer believe he or she can properly represent you, you can send a more formal termination email or letter. In this case, include your reasons for terminating the agreement, such as the rep's lack of performance. If the rep has met with someone, but you still have reasons to terminate the arrangement, such as the rep not informing you about meetings and schedule changes, you can similarly outline the reasons for termination. But explain that if anything comes of any meetings he or she has had, you will honor the agreement and pay any commissions that are due.

Normally, in these short term commission only arrangements, there is no need for lawyers to get involved. The rep didn't do the job; there is no commission due; and you and the rep have ended any relationship on the project. So you can both move on.

CHAPTER 10: DEBRIEFING THE REPS AND FOLLOWING-UP ON THEIR LEADS

Finally, it's time to follow-up, after your reps have worked on an assignment, event, or ongoing arrangement. If they have been a rep for a particular assignment or event, follow up within a week or two by phone, email, or a Skype call with out of town reps, or in person with reps in your area. If reps are working for you an ongoing basis, plan on meeting every week or two to go over what they have accomplished.

Following are some of the things to do in these follow-up meetings or email exchanges.

Get a List of Who the Rep Contacted with What Result

You may already have a list of who the reps were supposed to contact, in many cases due to a referral by you

Now you want a more complete list of who they actually met with and the result. In some cases, reps can close a deal by selling a product or service, and you need this contact information so you can follow through by delivering what they sold. In other cases, the reps have opened the door, and you have to use your expertise to close the sale.

The basic information to get from your reps includes the following:
- Date of Contact
- Name of Company
- Main Activities
- Name of Contact
- Title
- Company Website
- Phone
- Email
- Other Contact or Ccontacts
- Phone
- Emil
- Current Projects of Interest
- Interests for Future Projects
- Additional Comments

I have included some examples from a report I got from one of my reps, which is the type of information to include, although I have deleted the identifying information and used some made up names to illustrate.

SAT. NOV. 4

ABC COMPANY – Distribution – www.abc.com.   John Jones, co-founder, producer/distributor, john@abccompany.com. 212-123-4567, cell 917-321-7654 – (has Masters in Bio-Psych!) Please email him.
"marketplace for films"; sales/purchase films since 2012; matches buyers/sellers; many documentaries; interested in 3 completed projects - Driver, etc.
    1. How much to option book "Living Longer" for development?
    2. Where and what distribution are you looking for?
    3. Who is 2nd tier actor in Infidelity?

DEF STUDIOS – Production/Acquisition/Sales – defstudios.com Judy Jones, Head of Development; (writer/producer); jones@defstudios.com. 818-123-4567.
Interested in scripts/writing, all genres; wants a "brilliant script" with living dialog, example: Bad Frank movie; wants recognizable characters, i.e. Dirty Harry (movie – Split); Interested in Aging and Healthcare issues – please email her.

GHI PICTURES – Worldwide Sales & Distribution – GhiPictures.com (short meeting; they were behind!) Sally Ann, CEO-President; sally@ghipictures.com. 800-123-4567; cell 818-321-7654 (Don Smith, Sales & Acquisitions. Exec. don@ghipictures.com. 800-123-4568; cell 818-321-7653) Interested in all 3 finished products. Show films on bus lines…like Greyhound/transport buses/vans?

JKL ENTERTAINMENT – Production-Consulting (? just selling their own film) jklentertainment.in – Ali Ditka, producer/director/consultant – jklentertainment123@gmail.com   (in Mumbai); see business cards.

MNO GOOD NEWS FILMS - Rick Williams – (faith-based) –not interested in anything

PQR LA HISPANO - Seeking Hispanic talent; social network, online connection - virtual film market; www.pqrlahispano.com. Will Franklin, Co-Founder and CFO. wfranklin@pqrlahispano.com. 760-123-4567; interested in screenwriters; connecting writers, directors, agents; sales/purchase projects?

    The following pages continued in a similar vein:

AFM FOLLOW-UP MEETINGS – PAGE 2 – 11-5-2017 Ima Representative, Rep

    With a half-dozen more listings.

AFM FOLLOW-UP, PAGE 3 (from Sunday, 11-5-17), cont. Ima Representative, Rep

    And still more listings.

Such listings provide the information you need for further follow-up, either by you contacting the lead directly or by having further discussion with your rep by phone, email, or in person. In some cases, this further discussion can help you better understand how to follow up with a particular individual, since your rep will have more notes and recollections of that meeting.

For example, one AFM rep listed one company, called here MNO Good News Films, as not interested in anything offered. But in our phone conversation, she gave me more input on her uncomfortable meeting with "Rick Williams," who was insulting and short with her, saying he was not interested in action adventure films. Instead, he was only interested in films featuring real people encountering and overcoming hurdles in life in order to leave viewers with an uplifting inspirational message. So that was good information about why Rick wasn't interested and typically, this knowledge might open a door for future films in this inspirational genre. But since Rick was so insulting and dismissive to our rep, as she reported, this was a warning sign that this wasn't the kind of person we wanted to work with. So even if we did an inspirational faith-based film in the future, we would not contact MNO Good News Films about it.

You can use the form on the following page to give your reps, so they can fill in whatever information they have gotten.

Besides using this information to follow up yourself, you can use this form to determine what commissions to pay for sales that result from your rep's contacts, based on what they did in making the initial contact (ie. just getting a contact name or having a meeting).

FOLLOW-UP REPORT ON CONTACTS MADE AT:

_____

Date of Contact:_____

Name of Company:_____

Main Activities/Interests:_____

Name of Contact:_____

Title:_____

Company Website:_____

Office Phone _____ Cell Phone:_____

Email:_____

Other Contacts:_____

Office Phone _____ Cell Phone:_____

Email:_____

Current Projects of Interest:_____

Interests for Future Projects:_____

Additional Comments:_____

_____

_____

_____

_____

Get Business Cards, Company Information, Sales Literature and Other Information

If sales reps get business cards, sales literature, or other information about the company or its products and services, they should pass that information on to you by providing you with originals or copies.

However, you don't want every last email exchange reps have with prospects, since you don't need all this information. You just want a summary of what a company interested in what you are offering wants and the appropriate contact information, so you can follow through, such as indicated on the Follow-Up Report Form.

As an example of what you don't want, one rep sent me two files from her phone that showed every exchange she had for over a week with two dozen clients, each file totaling about 200 pages. But no, I didn't want to see 400 pages of back and forth exchanges in which she pitched the films, tried to set up appointments, and got replies. So ultimately, she sent back the lists of contacts with a short overview of what happened, such as listed on the previous page of examples, and that was perfect for me to follow-up.

This information about the company and its interests can help you consider different ways to work with different companies. Also, when you see examples of what other companies have been doing, this can give you ideas for new products or services to pitch to them. Thus, encourage your reps to collect and pass such information on to you.

Have a Personal or Group Meeting

In addition to getting written materials from the rep, have a follow-up personal meeting -- in person if your rep is local or set up a meeting by phone or Skype. This way, you develop a personal connection with your reps.

This contact also provides a way for the rep to give you additional feedback and for you to offer support and motivation to work with you on future projects if you need a rep.

In this meeting, some things to do are:
- go over your reactions to the material the rep has collected,
- ask the rep for any further needed information,
- learn more about the event the rep attended,
- answer any questions the rep has,
- find out about any difficulties the rep faced, so you can make the process smoother in the future,

- explain how you will be doing follow-up and keep the rep informed about the results.
- figure out any commissions due based on any sales resulting from the rep's efforts,
- discuss other relevant topics that come up during the conversation.

Following Up on Sales

If the reps have closed any sales of products or services, now it's up to you to follow up, provide those products or services, and pay the reps' commissions for their sales. You can use the form on the following page to keep track of any sales and handling fulfillment. This form indicates any commission due, which you should pay within 10 days of getting paid yourself.

If the sales rep has received a check for a product or serve, cash that, and arrange for delivery once that goes through. If it's a credit card sales, enter the card information, and ship the product or provide the service. Then, assuming no problems with the sale, pay the rep the agreed upon commission.

Following Up on Leads

If the rep has provided you with leads, organize these leads and follow through. Generally, when you are starting out, you will be the one with the knowledge and expertise, so you have to do this follow-through yourself. But over time, as you become more experienced and successful, you may be able to train others to follow through for you. Then, you take care of the close, unless you have trained others to do this.

For now, figure that you are responsible for following up yourself.

To this end, go through the contact information provided by your reps and note the prospects who are interested in further discussing what you are offering. You can attach a follow-up sheet to the information provided by your rep, whether on the Follow-Up Report on Contacts Form or on a list of information on contacts provided by the rep. In either case, note down the extent of contact the rep had with this prospect, from getting a card or referral to having an extended discussion. Then, rate this level of contact from 1 to the number of levels in your commission arrangement -- commonly from 3 to 5 steps. If a sale later goes through, you will know what commission to pay.

If prospects aren't interested, you might include them in a database for follow-up after 6 months to a year to see if circumstances have changed and if they might be interested in what you are developing now. Perhaps they may be.

89

In adding this information to a database, indicate the rep who made this initial contact and their level of contact, so you can credit them with a commission if anything comes through.

When you follow up, you can make your notes on the Follow-Up Report Form or list of information from your rep. As you prefer, attach more extensive notes on the Report Form or list. If you find on follow-up that the prospect isn't interested, note that, and if there is hope for the future, add this name to your database for future contacts.

If the prospect could be a good potential for either current or future projects, create a Follow-Up Form so you can add specific details on what the prospect is interested in and what you should do to follow up.

FOLLOW-UP RE[PRT FORM FOR CONTACTS AT:

_____

Name of Rep Making Contact_____ Commission Level____

Date of Initial Contact:_____ Date of Follow-Up Contact_____

Name of Company:_____

Main Activities/Interests:_____

Name of Contact:_____

Title:_____

Company Website:_____

Office Phone _____Cell Phone:_____

Email:_____

Other Contacts:_____

Office Phone_____ Cell Phone:_____

Email:_____

Projects of Current Interest:_____

Nature of Interest:_____

Type of Offer:_____

Interests for Future Projects:_____

Additional Comments:_____

_____

_____

Finally, provide any additional information the prospect needs to consider what you are offering and agree to your terms or come back to you with an offer. The way to do this depends on your industry and your product, service, or program.

For example, in the film industry, interested prospects will ask for more information, such as viewing a screener before making an offer, unless you have big name actors. Then, the name of the production company and the actors involved will often be enough.

In another industry, you may be given a RFP or request for proposal which indicates what you need to submit to have your project considered. Or sometimes you will be asked to submit a proposal. Then, submit the type of proposal common for that industry.

Whatever the procedures, submit the required materials or proposal. And after that, an interested prospect will either submit an offer or agree to your proposal, though now you may have to negotiate about particular terms and conditions. The specifics of this follow-up phase is beyond the scope of this book. You might review some books in your industry or about negotiations and contracts generally to better know what to do.

Still another option is to bring in a lawyer versed in your industry to help you decide what to do. The lawyer can act as an advisor or handle the negotiations and contract for you. Look to common practices in your industry, and be sure any lawyer you bring in is familiar with that field, so he or she doesn't recommend any negotiation tactics or claims out of line with common practices in your industry, since they could undermine your negotiations by being unrealistic or overly demanding.

Keeping the Rep Informed About the Results of Your Follow Up

As you follow-up on the leads from a rep, keep the rep informed about the result.

One way to keep the rep in the loop is when you engage in an email exchange with a prospect. You can simply send a copy to the rep. Should a prospect turn you down or want more information, the rep can see what is going on. However, once you enter into negotiations, it may be best to keep those between you, any partners, and the prospect. Afterwards, you can let the rep know the outcome, along with any commission if the lead turns into a sale. If you get a contract offer or sign one with the prospect, let the rep know.

Alternatively, let the rep know about who you are contacting, with what results. This is an especially common way to keep the rep informed if the follow-up involves phone calls or meetings.

Generally, you will get the no's fairly quickly, and you can let the rep know when you do or provide a regular update, perhaps once a week or bi-monthly, whatever the typical speed of decision-making in your industry.

If prospects are interested, decisions typically take longer, especially if decisions have to go through a number of parties in a larger company. So let the rep know about any project that remains under consideration. At least the rep can feel encouraged that his or her efforts led to some continued interest.

Then, if you turn a lead into a sale, agreement, job, or other arrangement, that's cause for celebration. Let the rep know as soon as possible and perhaps celebrate together.

Sometimes an agreement might not result in an immediate payout to anyone, as is often the case in the film industry, where you get an agreement for distribution, and the distributor typically covers the marketing costs and deducts these before anyone else is paid. But then, the rep should already understand this possibility of deductions from a payout from your initial conversations about repping you, as discussed in the chapter on recruiting reps. For example, the rep should understand if there are no initial returns but the commission payout could be very large, once you receive a return on the project. Just be sure reps understand how things work in your industry, so they know when and how a commission will be paid once a connection they make turns into a successful sale or agreement.

Working Out and Paying Commissions

If the lead turns into a sale or contract, let the rep know and indicate what the commission will be when the funds come through. Plan to pay the rep any commission due within 10 days of getting the funds.

For example, as of this writing, about four weeks after the AFM, our co-production team, Changemakers Productions and Dear Skyyler Productions, received a dozen distribution offers, and several contacts have been interested in developing documentaries or scripts for feature films. Depending on which deals we accept, a commission will be due. But if my partners already set up the meetings with the companies that lead to deals, there would be no commission paid on those.

If the rep provided the lead which turned into an offer, the rep would get a commission based on their commission level (ie: ranging from 1%-2 ½% based on their degree of contact -- from getting a card or name for follow-up to having an extended conversation). Alternatively, if the rep provided a lead but my partners separately arranged to meet with that company, the rep will get a half commission, as happened in one case. My rep met with the Acquisitions Director, while my partners met with the President. My partners also included that company on a list of companies not to contact about current projects, since they already set up a meeting with that company. But I forwarded that information to my rep and my rep set up a meeting, before I got the memo. As a result, since the Acquisitions Director has been corresponding with me in making an offer and sending the contract, it is unclear which contacts or maybe both led to the offer. Thus, if we accept this offer, the rep will get half the regular commission, since as in the insurance industry, when you are unsure about fault and liability in an accident, such as a parking lot fender bender, you split the difference, so it's 50-50 fault arrangement. Likewise, we will apply the same principle in paying half the commission to the rep.

CHAPTER 11: SUMMING UP AND MOVING ON

The Basic Steps to Follow

There you have it -- how to create and coordinate your first sales team. To review, the basic steps are:

1) Decide if you need one or more sales reps to pitch what your company is doing. Start small, and as you see what works, you can build your team and be even more successful in coordinating and supporting them and getting more sales.

2) Find your first sales reps through various means, including contacting family members, relatives, friends, and business associates; going to business networking and referral groups; attending Meetups and interest groups; and placing ads and announcement in the local media and online forums.

3) Create the sales and promotional materials you need to present your program and recruit your sales reps.

4) Develop your commission arrangements and contracts, so you are clear how you will
pay your sales reps, and it is clear what you expect them to do. Preferably start off with commission only contracts; though you may get fewer individuals interested in being reps, those you recruit may be more committed and effective in making sales, because that's how they get paid. Alternatively consider a small draw against commissions, especially if you are recruiting repos for ongoing projects.

5) Determine what you want to say to explain what prospective reps will do and what you want to ask reps in interviews.

6) Set up your interviews and talk to the reps by phone or in person to learn about the prospect's interests, background, and skills.

7) Hire your reps as independent contractors rather than employees and understand the difference, so you don't run afoul of employment regulations.

8) Create the necessary guidelines and other documents, so your reps have the materials they need to represent you.

9) Make sure that your reps provide you with reports of who they have met with what result, so you can follow through with leads or provide services and products for sales.

10) Coordinate what your reps are doing in the field by letting them find their own leads; assigning territories, days, or times; or providing referrals so reps can meet with those you refer.

11) Recognize when reps aren't working out and take immediate steps to get them to do what they should or terminate the agreement. As feasible, find a replacement or transfer their leads to another rep.

12) Get a list of who your reps contacted, so you can follow up by providing the products and services that were sold ot by contacting leads about their interests, so you can respond accordingly, and where possible, obtain contracts and close deals.

13) Let the reps know what you are doing to follow-up.

14) Arrange to pay any commissions when they are due, after you are paid for products, services, or projects resulting from the rep's contacts in representing you.

What's Next

Learn from your experiences in creating your first sales team. Make a note of what worked and what didn't, so when you hire reps in the future, you will hire and coordinate an even more effective team.

For future projects, try to hire the reps who have performed well. If any reps didn't perform as well as expected, discuss any problems with them to determine if they will seek to do a better job in the future. If so, consider giving them another chance if they are interested in working with you again. Or if they aren't interested in taking any steps to improve, don't hire them for anything else, even if they express interest in working with you on future projects.

And ideally, bring on even more reps for your next projects or to work with your company on an ongoing basis, so you can grow your company even more.

APPENDIX

SALES MATERIAL

CHANGEMAKERS PRODUCTIONS FILMS AVAILABLE FOR DISTRIBUTION

Following are brief descriptions of each of the films that are available for distribution, along with some information on our company and the co-producer we have worked with on these films. We are especially interested in a distributor or sales agent who can handle multiple films, though agreements for individual films are available. Also, worldwide rights are available, and we can work out agreements for selected territories. Please contact us for further information and to see screeners of these films.

Driver

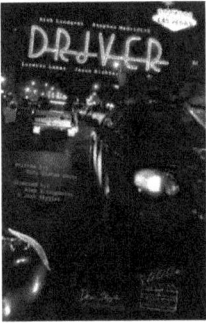

STARRING: **Stephen Medvidick** & **Rick Lundgren**
CO-STARRING: **Lorenzo Lamas (*Falcon Crest*) & Jason James Richter (*Free Willy, High and Outside*)**
PRODUCTION: Feature Film
GENRE: Suspense/Drama
SYNOPSIS: a dark drama about a Uber-like driver who becomes a serial killer.

ADDITIONAL INFORMATION: More specifically, *Driver* is about a Uber-like driver who becomes a serial killer and the cop who tracks him down. Among the stars are Lorenzo Lamas, the star of *Falcon Crest*, a Golden Globe winning TV show; Jason Richter, a star in Disney's $200 million dollar *Free Willy* franchise and more recently in *High and Outside*; Stephen Manley from *Star Trek*, and Aaron Strong, from the new Bourne film starring Matt Damon. So we're on our way for this to become a big hit! You can see the film on IMDB (International Movie Database) at http://www.imdb.com/title/tt5240090. A Facebook pagewith photos from the film shoot is at "driverthefilm." The trailer is on Changemakers Production's YouTube channel https://youtu.be/4doB44BGMCI
IMDB: http://www.imdb.com/title/tt5240090

Infidelity (Available December 2017)

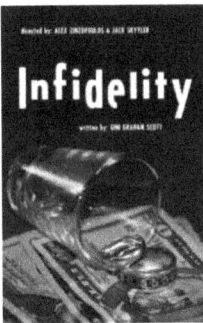

STARRING: **Jason James Richter and a second actor TBA**
PRODUCTION: Feature Film
GENRE: Suspense/Drama
SYNOPSIS: a suspense thriller about three couples who meet for dinner, when a mysterious caller threatens a bomb unless secrets are revealed.

ADDITIONAL INFORMATION: *Infidelity,* filmed February 8-20 and November 10-11 in Las Vegas, is in post-production. It's about three couples who come together for a dinner, after having worked together at a software company. They have many hidden secrets from each other, including husbands and wives cheating on each other, and one of them has embezzled from the company. Then, a mysterious caller says there is a bomb in the house and they must reveal certain secret

information. They can't leave or use their phones or the bomb will go off. But is this a bomber who knows them or a random prank caller? It's a psychological horror suspense film, with unexpected reveals and twists. Trailer and screener expected in December.
End of Life (Available in December)

PRODUCTION: Documentary
GENRE: Medical Day-in-the-Life Experience and Interviews
SYNOPSIS: a doctor specializing in end of life care features the doctor's day to day experiences as he takes care of patients and interacts with their family members and doctors, nurses, a palliative care team, and other medical professionals. The documentary also features interviews with family members and other medical professionals.
    ADDITIONAL INFORMATION: Filmed in February in Massachusetts. Final edits in postproduction to be completed in December 2017.

Changemakers Productions

The writer/executive producer of these films and TV series, Gini Graham Scott has a long history of successes in publishing and writing. She has published over 50 books with major publishers and has published over 100 books through her publishing company, Changemakers Publishing. She has written and produced over 60 short films and has 65 audio books on Audible which have sold over 800 copies in nine months. She also writes, ghostwrites, and promotes books and film scripts for others. You can see more about her and her company at her IMDB page and websites: http://www.imdb.com/name/nm2592609 www.changemakerspublishingandwriting.com and www.changemakersproductions.com, and www.ginigrahamscott.com.

Dear Skyyler Productions

The director and co-producer of these films and TV series is Jack Skyyler, the head of Dear Skyyler Productions. He has produced five other films, TV series, and documentaries with Changemakers Productions which include: *Suicide Party #Save Dave, Death's Door, Social Girl*, and *End of Life.* He won a REMI and two Best Director awards for his first feature *Hitting the Wall.* Other films which he wrote, produced, and directed include*: Night Aboard the Salem, Isabel: A Love Story, Skookum: The Hunt for the Bigfoot, Death of Love*, and *Infested Ship.* Most recently he produced and directed *The Haunted Ship*, a $2 million production scheduled for release in 2015.

Contact Information:

TV PROJECT AVAILABLE FOR DISTRIBUTION

Following is a brief description of a TV series available for purchase. Worldwide rights are available, and we can work out agreements for selected territories. Please contact us for further information.

Death's Door

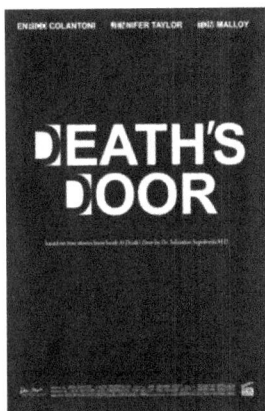

STARRING: Enrico Colantoni (*Flashpoint*), Jennifer Taylor (*Two and a Half Men*), Ellen Hollman (*Spartacus*), Catherine Mary Stewart (*Weekend at Bernie's*), and Alfonso Freeman (*Shawshank Redemption*)
PRODUCTION: TV Pilot
GENRE: Medical Drama
SYNOPSIS: *Death's Door* is a medical drama based on the book *At Death's* **Door**, the true-life story of **Sebastian Sepulveda M.D.** *Death's Door* tells the story of Dr. Mark Corbin, a doctor whose entire career has been spent dealing with the terminally ill and dying. We see the struggle to face death and the havoc it creates on everyone around him: patients, loved ones, family, and hospital staff.

ADDITIONAL INFORMATION: *Death's Door* is a first episode for a TV series based on the experiences of a doctor, Sebastian Sepulveda, who specializes in end-of-life care. The series is based on the book *At Death's Door*, co-authored with Gini Graham Scott, which was published by Rowman & Littlefield in March 2017. *Death's Door* was filmed at a hospital in Massachusetts with some major actors, including Enrico Colantoni, who was in *Veronica Mars, Person of Interest,* and *Just Shoot Me!,* and Jennifer Taylor, who was in *Waterboy* and *Two and a Half Men.* The filming got major press coverage with a two page spread with a gallery of photos and 5 video clips. A press release about this feature is at http://www.expertclick.com/NewsRelease/-Filming-of-At-Deaths-Door-Featured-in-Massachusetts-Press-,201681183.aspx and the original article is at http://www.sentinelandenterprise.com/news/ci_30157086/life-and-death-drama. A Facebook page is at "atdeathsdoorbookandfilm." A documentary based on the experiences of the doctor called *End of Life* was filmed in December 2016. The trailer is on the Changemakers Production YouTube channel at https://youtu.be/oDzrca6WLNQ.
    IMDb: http://www.imdb.com/title/tt5631642
For further information and a private link to a screener, contact us.

Contact Information:

SCRIPTS AVAILABLE FOR SALE OR CO-PRODUCTION

Following are brief descriptions of the next scripts we plan to raise funds for filming from co-producers and investors. The scripts are also for sale to producers. These will be our 6th film and TV projects from Changemakers Productions and Dear Skyyler Productions. Contact us for further information

BRAIN SWAP: a sci-fi legal/crime action drama (March 2018)
Sam, a wealthy businessman, whose life and health are failing, seeks a new life through a brain transplant into a dying criminal. As Jack, he marries and becomes a respected community leader, until a TV story leads to his arrest for murder. His trial becomes a media circus about who he is - Jack, Sam, or the criminal – with unexpected results.
Script trailer: http://www.youtube.com/watch?v=BO34PiMsveo

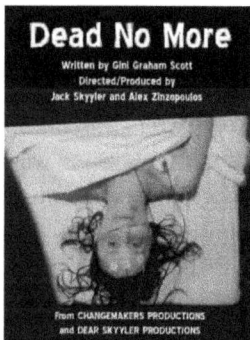

DEAD NO MORE: a sci-fi suspense thriller (April 2018)
After a lawyer wins a dispute and acquires a cryonics tank with a shrewish wealthy woman frozen for 20 years, a scientist friend brings her back. It turns out her husband "killed" her and her children took her property. When the lawyer tries to regain her property, her husband tries to kill her again, as she transforms into a nice person in her 50s. The *Dead No More* Short won 2 awards at a Castro Theater Film Festival March 2013 in SF.
Script Trailer: http://www.youtube.com/watch?v=dG057_926l0;
Sizzle Reel: http://www.youtube.com/watch?v=zx-nanJqFRE.

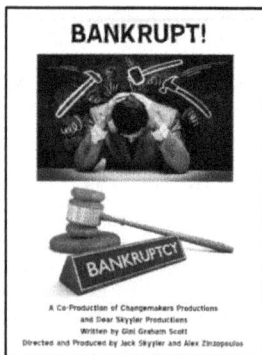

BANKRUPT, a suspense, action drama (June 2018)
A bankruptcy attorney is going bankrupt because not enough people are filing for bankruptcy as the economy improves, so he turns to crime. But then, one of his fraud victims gets help from one of his underpaid employees, a recent law school graduate specializing in criminal justice, and soon his crimes escalate as he struggles to avoid getting caught.

Out of Control: an action/mystery thriller - inspired by a true story
After a woman's car breaks down in the desert and a parking lot battle escalates, she investigates and discovers all kinds of illegal activities from consumer scams to immigration fraud, chop shop operations, and murder. Soon she has to evade the scammers and killers and seek justice with the help of associates, police, and FBI.
Script Trailer for the parking lot conflict:
http://www.youtube.com/watch?v=0QEEWmMX8wk
Sizzle Reel: http://www.youtube.com/watch?v=iUalPgJmPTA

The New Child: a sci-fi contemporary suspense drama
An archaeologist and his wife can't have a child, when he discovers a 15,000 year-old skeleton and uses its DNA in a cloning experiment to have a child, which he and his wife raise as their own. But the child becomes increasingly wild leading to media frenzy.
Script trailer: http://www.youtube.com/watch?v=mMs0ysJnRyk.

Coke and Diamonds: a legal/crime action thriller - inspired by a true story
A federal prosecutor matches wits with an international drug trafficker posing as an importer, who charms a jury, escapes prison, and enters high society. When the prosecutor pursues him with an FBI agent using surveillance, stings, undercover agents, informants, wiretaps, and a hotel raid, he nearly loses the case, his job, and reputation, but succeeds due to an unexpected clue.

Rich and Dead: an action/suspense/mystery thriller, based on a true story
After a homicide secretary's wealthy friend, seeking divorce, becomes ill, the secretary suspects the woman's husband of poisoning her. After her friend's death, with help from her boyfriend and a homicide detective, she prevents a cremation and foils efforts to dispose of the body, leading to a chase through an abandoned shipyard and the capture of two gunman and the husband.

Deadly Affair: a cop/action/mystery thriller
After a beat cop with marriage problems has an affair with a neighborhood activist battling drug dealers, she turns up dead, and he could be the suspect. He turns to his brother-in-law, a homicide investigator, to find the real killer, and they risk death as their investigation leads to a vacation retreat in the mountains.

Turn Around: a Romeo-Juliet type of story set in a near future where racial roles are reversed Blacks and Hispanics have power and political offices, while whites are low-income underdogs. A wealthy black teen falls for a poor white girl in high school and mayhem ensues.

Contact Information:

FILM PROJECTS UNDER DEVELOPMENT
ON LIVING A LONGER HEALTHIER LIFE

Following are brief descriptions of the documentary film projects for which we will be raising funds from investors or are seeking co-producers. Alternatively, we can develop these projects for a producer or production company. The co-developer Gini Graham Scott has written and produced 6 film and TV projects through Changemakers Productions and Dear Skyyler Productions, and these documentaries can be developed through this co-production or through other arrangements. One of these documentaries is based on a book by Scott published by ABC-Clio: *The Science of Living Longer.* The other co-developer is Linda Meneken. Contact us for further information.

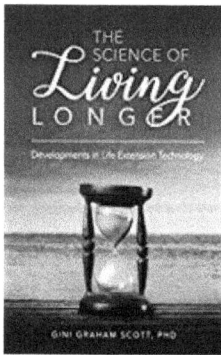

The Science of Living Longer: Developments in Life Extension Technology by Gini Graham Scott, Ph.D. provides a fascinating look at the current state of the scientific research on how people can live significantly longer—and possibly forever. The book begins with an introductory section on the historical efforts to achieve immortality in Western and other cultures. Following chapters investigate different strands of research on achieving a longer life or even immortality. Other chapters address topics such as the health, wellness, and fitness movements to help individuals live longer; the biological methods—such as cell rejuvenation—to defeat aging; and the development of an exoskeleton as body parts age. Each chapter also suggests steps an individual can take to live longer. To be published by ABC-Clio in December 2017.

The Secrets of Healthy Aging. This how-to documentary, developed by Gini Graham Scott with Linda Meneken, a physical therapist for a company specializing in services for older adults, provides an overview of the major techniques to live a healthy, longer life. It features interviews with experts in the field, including doctors, coaches, and others, along with a look at the lives of healthy older individuals, based on interviews about their everyday life. A companion book is being developed, too.

Profiles in Healthy Aging: Featuring Individuals of 90 and Older Living Active Lives. Today, older individuals live longer than ever -- and they are living very active, healthy lives. Some even have more energy and are more productive than many individuals in their 20s and 30s. This documentary features an overview of the major characteristics of these much older healthy individuals and the attitudes and activities that keep them young. Then, it features 25 profiles of 90+ individuals, based on interviews and a videographer following them around in their daily life. A companion book is also being developed.

Contact Information:

BACKGROUND INFORMATION

INTRODUCING CHANGEMAKERS PRODUCTIONS AND DEAR SKYYLER PRODUCTIONS

Following is an introduction to Changemakers Productions and Dear Skyyler Productions, who have co-produced a half-dozen film and TV projects. These include:

Suicide Party #Save Dave (distributed by RSquared Films)

Driver (just completed; available for distribution)

Social Girl (script sold, filming September 21-October 5, 2017)

Infidelity (initial filming February 2017; final filming November 10-11, 2017)

Death's Door (TV pilot, based on the book *At Death's Door,* available for distribution)

End of Life (documentary, available for distribution December 2017).

We are interested in contacting mangers, agents, producers, distributors, sales agents, and investors to work with us on various projects. We are open to work with individuals interested in repping or producing all of our projects or in splitting arrangements up by project and territories. Please contact us for further information

Changemakers Productions

The writer/executive producer of these films and TV series, Gini Graham Scott, has a long history of successes in publishing and writing. She has published over 50 books with major publishers, has published over 100mbooks through her own publishing company, has written and produced over 60 short films, has 58 audio books on Audible which have sold over 700 copies in seven months, and she writes and ghostwrites books and film scripts for others. You can see more about her and her company on IMDB at http://www.imdb.com/name/nm2592609 or on her company and individual websites at www.changemakerspublishingandwriting.com and www.changemakersproductions.com.

Dear Skyyler Productions

The director and co-producer is Jack Skyyler, the head of Dear Skyyler Productions, who won a REMI and two Best Director awards for his first feature *Hitting the Wall.* Other films which he wrote, produced, and directed include*: Night Aboard the Salem, Isabel: A Love Story, Skookum: The Hunt for the Bigfoot, Death of Love*, and *Infested Ship*. Most recently he produced and directed *The Haunted Ship*, a $2 million production scheduled for release in 2015.

Contact Information:

COMMISSION ARRANGEMENT AND CONTRACT

Here's an example of our commission arrangement. It started off as a draft and was finalized after the first prospective reps provided their comments.

AFM Arrangements for Commissions
For Representing Changemakers Productions at the AFM

Following are the arrangements for commissions for the sale of any of these completed films, TV series, or documentary or for the sale of any scripts or proposed films or documentaries. There will also be other opportunities for work on completed projects, including promotion and events, and for future projects, such as fundraising, being in the film, assisting on set, and getting involved with promotion and events once the project is completed. Here are current arrangements based on sharing my commission for these two types of sales.

Sales of a Completed Project to or by a Distributor or Sales Agent

There are two types of sales. In one case, there may be an upfront payment; in other cases, the payment will come from a royalty based on quarterly, bi-annual, or annual sales. A 5% commission, which is basically a finders fee. You will be paid based on finding the distributor or sales agent, and it will be paid on the top before the investors are paid back their investment plus 20, after which the producers and investors will share in the returns. So this commission could take the form of an upfront payment or continuing payment. Your share of the 5% commission will be as follows:

1% for an initial conversation with a potentially good match for follow-up.

1 ½% for a more extended initial conversation, where you take some time to give out literature and get information for follow-up.

2% where you have a meeting based on an appointment which I have set up based on a mailing to exhibitors or AFM attendees

2 ½% where you set up the meeting after an initial conversation with an exhibitor or a meeting at the pool, hotel lobby, or other venue.

You can indicate which this is when you send me the contact form with information about the company, your meeting, and what they are interested in.

Sales of a Script or Proposed Documentary or TV Series

In this case, the sale often will take the form of an upfront advance payment followed by a schedule of payments as the project is completed or a payment upon completion, and then there may be future earnings on the project. This kind of sale is like that made by an agent, where the standard commission in the industry is 10%, so you will be sharing that with me. The share of the 10%

commission will be structured much like the previous set up for selling a completed project, except the percent will be double. For example:

2% for an initial conversation with a potentially good match for follow-up.

3% for a more extended initial conversation, where you take some time to give out literature and get information for follow-up.

4% where you have a meeting based on an appointment which I have set up based on a mailing to exhibitors or AFM attendees

5% where you set up the meeting after an initial conversation with an exhibitor or a meeting at the pool, hotel lobby, or other venue.

You can indicate which this is when you send me the contact form with information about the company, your meeting, and what they are interested in.

And here's a copy of the contract.

AFM Agreement
For Representing Changemakers Productions at the AFM

It is understood that you will be representing Changemakers Productions headed up by Gini Graham Scott at the American Film Market during the event from November 1-8 on a non-exclusive basis, along with anything else you may be doing at the AFM. The purpose of this representation is to present film and TV projects to distributors, sales agents, producers, investors, and other contacts who may be interested in projects from Changemakers Productions, many of which are co-productions with Dear Skyyler Productions. In particular, these activities will include:

1) Obtaining an AFM pass for at least one day.

2) Meeting with exhibitors, which may include distributors, sales agents, and producers, and with others at the event.

3) Providing contacts with the relevant flyers about Changemakers' projects.

4) Printing up copies of the flyers from PDF files.

5) Obtaining business cards or other information from the individuals contacted, so that Changemakers Productions can follow with that individual or referral for future contact.

6) These meetings may be brief and simply involve introducing yourself, explaining that you are representing Changemakers Productions (apart from anything else you might be pitching), and giving the contacts the relevant flyers. These flyers include flyers on Films for Distribution, TV Series for Distribution, Available Film Scripts, Projects on Living Longer and Healthy Aging, Proposals for Documentaries, and an Introduction to Changemakers Productions and Skyyler Productions.

7) Keeping a list of those contacted with information for follow-up using the AFM Contact Sheet to be provided to you as a .docx or Excel form. This information will include the name of the person contacted, their title, any referral to another contact, their title, the contact and/or referral's email and phone number, and what they are interested in.

8) Providing a copy of this list to Changemakers Productions after the AFM, and phoning Changemakers Productions about any contacts who should be contacted during the AFM.

9) Asking for any assistance needed with follow-up during the AFM.

In return, you will be getting the following from Changemakers Productions

1) Files of the flyers to be shown to contacts

2) Guidelines about what to say to introduce yourself and the types of projects you are repping for Changemakers Productions; and then what to say to under various scenarios

3) A list of exhibitors and others who have expressed interest in being contacted at the show (along with their room numbers as available)

4) A breakdown of the list of exhibitors to contact, so these are distributed between the 3 team members contacting people at the show (i.e.: broken down by day or by floor)

5) A form to use to keep track of contact information and provide it to Changemakers Productions.

6) The basic financial arrangement is that you will share in the finders' fee which comes off the top of any money's received for either distributing or purchasing the film, documentary, or TV series or purchasing or investing in one of the scripts or proposed documentaries or TV series.

7) The finders' fee for distribution or purchasing the film is 5%, and you will receive from 1-2 1/2% depending on what you do, from simply collecting a card from a contact to having a more in-depth meeting about these projects, as outlined in the more detailed breakdown of these arrangements. The finders' fee for purchasing or investing in one of the scripts is 10% (the same as WGA agents get for selling scripts), and you will receive 2-5% of this depending on what you do, from collecting a card for future contact to having a meeting with the contact, as outlined in the more detailed breakdown of these arrangements.

8) Changemakers Productions will keep you informed about the results of the follow-up with the contacts you have provided and advise you about any agreements that result, and you will share accordingly in the financial return.

9) I have sent an e-mail to AFM exhibitors and will send an email to approximately 1500 attendees who are part of the MyAFM database, and you can access that as well to see who might be interested in scripts and proposed

documentaries and TV series. I will be forwarding contact information to members of the AFM team to contact at the AFM.

You are free to contact anyone about your own projects apart from any individual contacts provided to you or appointments set up for you by Changemakers Productions, as long as you make it clear when you are acting as a rep for Changemakers Productions and when you are acting in your own behalf. These individual contacts are the ones provided to you through an email, phone call, or one-on-one meeting; this does not include anyone on the AFM list of exhibitors or attendees who you contact directly yourself.

_____   _____
  For Changemakers Productions   For AFM Rep

_____   _____
           Date   Date

GUIDELINES FOR AFM REPS

Here's an example of the detailed guidelines which I prepared for the reps, so they would know what to do and so I could incorporate any requirements, expectations, and compensation in the guidelines into a formal agreement.

AFM Guidelines
For Representing Changemakers Productions at the AFM

Following are guidelines for what to do and say at the AFM under various scenarios.

In General:

1. You can call yourself a "rep," "representative," or "liaison" for Changemakers Productions as you prefer in presenting Changemakers Productions materials or in asking for information for Changemakers Productions.

3. Think of yourself as just finding out information on who is interested in what and/or opening the door for further discussion with prospective distributors, sales agents, film producers, production companies, and other potentially interested industry professionals. You don't need to do any more than obtain that information and open the doors. After that, I, Alex, or Jack will handle any follow-up.

2. Just be familiar with the material in the flyers about the various film projects and Changemakers Productions and Skyyler Productions. If there are questions beyond the information you already have or an interest in seeing any screeners or trailers, refer that to me for follow-up -- or to Jack or Alex at the show if these seem to be seriously interested in distribution. Those who are interested can see any trailers described in the introductory flyers, but for screeners, I, Jack, or Alex need to follow-up with them first, so we know who is gaining access to these password protected screeners and we want to prescreen those expressing interest to make sure these are.

Meetings to Avoid or Explain Where Jack or Alex Already Have Meetings

There are about a dozen distributors and sales agents where Jack and Alex have already set up meetings. I sent out a query to exhibitors before this list was available. Some distributors and sales agents advised me that they already have meetings. In other cases, I might get a response for a meeting with someone else in the company, or you might happen to meet that person. I will be attaching a list of individuals and companies not to contact.

In the event a meeting should have been scheduled or you should encounter someone on the list, just explain that you are working with Changemakers Productions that is working with Jack Skyyler Productions, so they should go over any completed films for productions with them. But if they are interested in participating in future feature films, documentaries, or TV series, you can talk to them about that. In any case, get their business card and make a note about any meeting so I can follow-up or let Jack and Alex know about the meeting.

Meetings for Appointments with Distributors, Sales Agents, and Others in Rooms

These will generally be 10-20 minute meetings, sometimes shorter or longer.

Just introduce yourself as a rep or liaison for Changemakers Productions, who will follow-up with them. Do the following in whatever order seems the most fitting.

If you don't already know, find out what types of projects they are most in and what they do (ie: distributor, sales rep, or other). Generally, distributors and sales reps will only be interested in completed films and maybe documentaries and TV projects. If they are also producers or production companies, they may be interested in the scripts, proposed documentaries, or TV projects.

Get their business card and any literature about their company and what they do. You can take notes on their cards, literature, or notepad.

Briefly highlight the projects on the flyers that they might be most interested in (ie: completed films, documentary, or TV series).

Briefly let them know about what Changemakers Productions does (writing, executive producer, and promotion for these projects) and what Dear Skyyler Productions does (filming, production, and post production) and maybe mention a few credits.

If they might be interested in any of these projects or future projects, give them the relevant flyers, including the bio sheet about Changemakers Productions and Dear Skyyler Productions.

Let them know that Gini Graham Scott of Changemakers Productions or Alex Zinzopoulos or Jack Skyyler of Dear Skyyler Productions will follow-up with them.

Make a note of what happened for follow-up. If not interested, note this too and why.

Meetings with Producers, Production Companies, Agents, and Others by Pool, in Lobby, and Other Areas

I will be sending out an email to AFM attendees tomorrow more to try to set up appointments which I will share among you. It may be better for you to schedule your meetings with them than for me to try to set something else. Feel free to share these requests for meetings with each other. If necessary, I can try to set something up, or talk to people on the phone if it is difficult to set up a meeting yourself -- or if they want to talk after the show. In any case, get a business card if you meet, or send me information on what happened so I can follow up.

You are also encouraged to meet with others at the pool, in the lobby, at off-site events, at happy hours and clubs, and the like. You can meet with them together, though ideally split up at the location and mix around. If two or more of you meet with someone, let me know who will be the primary contact for when I handle any follow-up.

- ### Initial Conversations

Often these will just be short conversations -- of about 1-5 minutes, where you exchange basic information -- find out who they are and what they are interested in, and give them a 30-60 second elevator pitch about the type of film and TV projects you are representing. Then, if there is interest in learning more, schedule another time to meet, or if that isn't possible, get their card and note what they are interested in so I can follow-up.

If you meet any distributors and sales   agents here, they will normally just be interested in completed films, so briefly talk about those.

120

If you meet any producers, production companies, agents, financiers, investors, or others, they will be interested in future projects, so you can brief mention the types of projects we are doing (scripts, documentaries, TV series) and then briefly tell them about the available projects in these types of projects.

If they want more information, you can set up a meeting to talk further, and then proceed as above at this meeting. If they don't have time for a meeting, just get their business card and note what they are interested in, so I can follow up.

- **Informational Meetings**

If the person you meet wants to set up a time to meet to discuss whatever they are interested in, you can set up a meeting if you can. Sometimes these might be after the event you are at or at another time, and if you can have a meeting great. Then proceed much as you would with a distributor or sales agent, except you will focus on the scripts or proposed documentaries or TV series. Just consider these informational meetings or open the door meetings, based on what you already know from the flyers. Let them know that I will handle follow-up. Here's a description of what to do adapted from the above lists of things to do in meeting with distributors and sales agents.

These will generally be 10-20 minute meetings, sometimes shorter or longer.

Just introduce yourself as a rep or liaison for Changemakers Productions, who will follow-up with them. Do the following in whatever order seems the most fitting.

If you don't already know, find out what types of projects they are most in and what they do. If they are producers, production companies, agents, financiers, or investors, they may be interested in the scripts, proposed documentaries, or TV projects.

Get their business card and any literature about their company and what they do. You can take notes on their cards, literature, or notepad.

Briefly highlight the projects on the flyers that they might be most interested in (ie: scripts, proposed documentaries, or TV projects).

Briefly let them know about what Changemakers Productions does (writing, executive producer, and promotion for these projects) and what Dear Skyyler Productions does (filming, production, and post production) and maybe mention a few credits.

If they might be interested in any of these projects, give them the relevant flyers, including the bio sheet about Changemakers Productions and Dear Skyyler Productions.

Let them know that Gini Graham Scott of Changemakers Productions will follow-up with them.

Make a note of what happened for follow-up. If not interested, note this and why.

Initial Contact with an Exhibitor (Generally a Distributor or Sales Agents, Some Also Producers)

Aside from meetings with appointments and people you meet at the pool, hotel lobby, and other locations, most of your meetings will be initial contacts with exhibitors that might lead to further conversations or future meetings. This is what I did when I went to one of the AFM events about 6 years ago -- just went up and down the floors and stopped in rooms and got cards for follow-up later. To this end, you each have 2 floors -- 3-4 - Linda; 5-6 - Charmane, and 7-8 - Brett. Since there are about 300 exhibitors, each floor will have about 50 exhibitors. Skip the rooms where I have already set up appointments for you (I will send you a list of these) or where Jack and Alex already have appointments (I will send you a list of these, too). There are about 20 of these so far. When you go into these rooms, do the following in whatever seems the most appropriate order:

- Briefly introduce yourself as a rep for Changemakers Productions, which has a slate of feature films, a documentary, and a TV series.

- Indicate that you would like to find out whoever handles new projects or acquisitions, and if possible you would like to arrange for a meeting here or the CEO of Changemakers Productions will follow-up with them later after the show.

- Find out the type of projects they do (sometimes this may be obvious from their posters in the room or sales literature)

- Find out if they are interested in the type of projects we are doing. Generally, they will only be interested in completed films, and possibly in TV series and documentaries. But also check if they get involved as a producer or co-producer in developing new projects, and if so, you can mention that we also have scripts and proposed documentaries and TV shows.

- If this seems like a good match, if possible set up a meeting to talk more about the projects on the slate, and then at that meeting, proceed as above.

- If this seems like a good match, but they aren't available for a meeting at the AFM, just get the information for follow-up by me, Alex, or Jack after the show.

- If not a good match, just indicate this.

- Get the business card of the individual to contact for follow-up and any company literature.

- Then, depending on their interest and availability do the following:
  - Set up a meeting if they might be interested and available
  - Refer them to me for follow-up if they might be interested but not available.
  - Refer them to me to eliminate them from further contact if not interested.
  - Record any information on the contact sheet, so I can follow-up if there is possible interest, or eliminate them from further follow-up if not a good match.

I think that's it. Have fun and feel free to pursue your own projects with any of the people you meet yourself, but just make it clear when you are being a rep for Changemakers Productions and when you are presenting your own project.

EXAMPLES OF LETTERS SENT TO GET LEADS FOR REPS

Here are examples of the letters I sent out to exhibitors and attendees.

To Exhibitors (Mostly Distributors and Sales Reps, and Some Service Providers)

Subject Line: Team with Suspense Thrillers, Medical TV Series, and Other Projects Seeks Meetings with Distributors, Sales Agents, Producers at AFM

Dear ********:

I am writing to you since we have a team of three people from our company Changemakers Productions who will be at the AFM, as will two directors/producers of most of our co-productions with Dear Skyyler Productions. We would like to set up meetings if you are interested in any of our current or future offerings, and I will handle follow-up after the AFM. Or if you are not able to arrange a meeting, I can contact you by email, phone, or Skype to discuss our projects.

Following are brief descriptions of each of the films, TV series, and documentaries that are available for distribution, along with some information on our company and the co-producer we have worked with on these films. We are especially interested in a distributor or sales agent who can handle multiple films, though agreements for individual films are available. Worldwide rights are available, and we can work out agreements for selected territories. We are also interested in contacting distributors or producers about working together on our future projects, which include scripts, documentaries, and TV series for which we are looking for co-producers.

I'm including information on the currently completed projects and can send you more information on our scripts and proposed documentaries and TV series. I can also send you links to screeners of current and previous projects.

Please contact me about the best times to set up meetings at the AFM and your location there, or contact me for further information on seeing screeners or one-sheets about our scripts and proposed documentaries, and TV series. Details on currently available projects are below. If you have already set up a meeting with Dear Skyyler Productions, you can contact them directly.

Sincerely,

Gini Graham Scott, Ph.D.
Writer/Executive Producer, Changemakers Productions
(and contact information)

Then the letter included additional information on the projects and Changemakers Productions

<u>To Attendees (Buyers, Producers, Investors, and Others, including Talent and Service Providers)</u>

Subject Line: Team of Production Company Reps Seek Meetings at the AFM with Co-Producers, Producers, and Others for Scripts, Documentaries, TV Series, and Developmental Projects

Dear ********:

I am writing to you since we have a team of three people from our company Changemakers Productions who will be at the AFM, as will two directors/producers of most of our co-productions with Dear Skyyler Productions. They will all be meeting with distributors and sales agents for our slate of 6 completed projects: four feature films, a documentary, and a TV series pilot. We have worked with Dear Skyyler Productions on these as the writer and executive producer. These projects include: *Suicide Party #Save Dave,* in distribution and for sale in over 200 venues; *Driver* and *Infidelity,* two suspense thrillers, *Death's Door,* a pilot for a TV series, and *End of* Life, a documentary about a doctor dealing with terminal patients, their families, and medical professionals.

We would also like to set up meetings about any of a half-dozen projects where we are looking for co-producers for scripts and documentaries for which we plan to raise funds, or we are looking for producers to take over the production of any of these projects. In addition, we are seeking producers for two TV-series based on successfully published books.

Our reps can also discuss how we might work together on other projects, since we do a lot of writing on assignment, should you have an idea you want to develop.

If you can set up a meeting, I will handle follow-up after the AFM. Or if you are not able to arrange a meeting, I can contact you by email, phone, or Skype to discuss our projects.

I can tell you more about these projects if you want more information or if you want to set up a meeting with one of our three reps who will be at the show from Nov. 3-7. I have included some information on our company below.

Sincerely,

Nancy Parker
Executive Assistant, Changemakers Productions

Then the letter included bio information about Changemakers Productions.

ABOUT THE AUTHOR

GINI GRAHAM SCOTT, Ph.D., J.D., is a nationally known writer, consultant, speaker, and seminar leader, specializing in business and work relationships, professional and personal development, social trends, and popular culture. She has published over 50 books with major publishers. She has worked with dozens of clients on memoirs, self-help, popular business books, and film scripts. Writing samples are at www.ginigrahamscott.com and www.changemakerspublishingandwriting.com. She is a Huffington Post regular columnist, commenting on social trends, business, and everyday life at www.huffingtonpost.com/gini-graham-scott.

She is the founder of Changemakers Publishing, featuring books on work, business, psychology, social trends, and self-help. It has published over 50 print, e-books, and audiobooks. She has licensed several dozen books for foreign sales, including the UK, Russia, Korea, Spain, and Japan.

She has received national media exposure for her books, including appearances on *Good Morning America, Oprah,* and *CNN*. She has been the producer and host of a talk show series, *Changemakers*, featuring interviews on social trends.

Her books on business relationships and professional development include:

Self-Publishing Secrets (Changemakers Publishing)
Turn Your Dreams into Reality (Llewellyn)
Resolving Conflict (Changemakers Publishing)
A Survival Guide for Working with Bad Bosses (AMACOM)
A Survival Guide for Working with Humans (AMACOM)
Credit Card Fraud with Jen Grondahl Lee (Rowman)
Lies and Liars: How and Why Sociopaths Lie (Skyhorse Publishing)

Scott is also active in a number of community and business groups, including the Lafayette, Pleasant Hill, and Danville Chambers of Commerce. She is a graduate of the prestigious Leadership Contra Costa program, is a7 member of two B2B groups in Danville and Walnut Creek, and a BNI member. She is the organizer of six Meetup groups in the film and publishing industries with over 6000 members in Los Angeles and the San Francisco Bay Area. She does workshops and seminars on the topics of her books.

She received her Ph.D. from the University of California, Berkeley, and her J.D. from the University of San Francisco Law School. She has received several MAs at Cal State University, East Bay.

CHANGEMAKERS PUBLISHING
3527 Mt. Diablo Blvd., #273
Lafayette, CA 94549
changemakers@pacbell.net . (925) 385-0608
www.changemakerspublishingandwriting.com